Modernism and Tradition in
Ernest Hemingway's In Our Time

Studies in American Literature and Culture

Edited by James Hardin
(*South Carolina*)

Ernest Hemingway, circa 1916.

Matthew Stewart

MODERNISM AND TRADITION IN ERNEST HEMINGWAY'S
In Our Time

A Guide for Students and Readers

CAMDEN HOUSE

First published 2001 by Camden House
Reprinted in paperback and transferred to digital printing 2009

Camden House is an imprint of Boydell & Brewer Inc.
668 Mt. Hope Avenue, Rochester, NY 14620, USA
www.camden-house.com
and of Boydell & Brewer Limited
PO Box 9, Woodbridge, Suffolk IP12 3DF, UK
www.boydellandbrewer.com

Hardback ISBN-13: 978–1–57113–017–4
Hardback ISBN-10: 1–57113–017–9
Paperback ISBN-13: 978–1–57113–412–7
Paperback ISBN-10: 1–57113–412–3

Library of Congress Cataloging-in-Publication Data

Stewart, Matthew, 1957–
    Modernism and tradition in Ernest Hemingway's In our time : a guide
for students and readers / Matthew Stewart
    p. cm. — (Studies in American literature and culture)
    Includes bibliographical references and index.
    ISBN 1–57113–017–9 (alk. paper)
    1. Hemingway, Ernest, 1899–1961. In our time.   2. Modernism
(Literature) — United States.   3. Adams, Nick (Fictitious character)
4. Literary form.   5. Short story.   I. Title.   II. Series
    PS3515.E37 153752001
    813'.52—dc21

                                                                00-064200

A catalogue record for this title is available from the British Library.

This publication is printed on acid-free paper.
Printed in the United States of America.

Cover image: Hemingway's passport, 1923. Photo EH 6143D,
courtesy of the John F. Kennedy Library, Boston.

For June Stewart, first of my teachers,

And in memory of Vernon Stewart,

A fine craftsman in his own right.

Contents

Acknowledgments

I extend my thanks to the editors at Camden House. I thank Jim Hardin for his interest and encouragement early on. Phil Dematteis's copyediting helped shape up the manuscript. Jim Walker deserves special thanks for being on top of everything that matters at each stage. He has managed the production beautifully. To friends and colleagues I also owe thanks. Milton Cohen saved me from errors, and asked stimulating questions. Robert Wexelblatt helped me see the real value of this project at a time when I needed to see it anew myself. Natalie McKnight has provided caring, committed leadership in my academic life and has been enormously helpful during a period that was much too busy (for both of us). John Fawell was there to talk about Hemingway's stories, to commiserate about the writing and publishing process and, most importantly, to make me laugh. Anne Barclay photocopied and typed like a trooper.

To my wife Judith Seltzer and to our son Jacob, I simply say that I can't imagine a day without you. What you've done along the way would take pages to acknowledge, but what you've been is even more important.

M. C. S.
September 2000

Foreword

THIS BOOK IS FOR READERS who wish to gain a deeper understanding of Ernest Hemingway's *In Our Time*. Though not as
widely known as his famous novels, such as *The Sun Also Rises*
(1926), *A Farewell to Arms* (1929), or *For Whom the Bell Tolls*
(1940), Hemingway's volume of interrelated short fictions continues
to gain new readers and to be taught in university courses. In some
important ways bolder and more radically experimental than his
most acclaimed novels, *In Our Time* is an artistic achievement of the
first order and one that may well leave even seasoned readers with
many unanswered questions. Just where do these brief, italicized
"Chapters" come from, and how do they fit in with the longer stories? Why is Nick Adams in so many of the stories but not in all?
Why are the stories so full of violence and death? While no book can
answer all such questions, I trust that this one provides some helpful
information and hope that it opens up avenues of thought for the
reader. While students, new instructors, and non-specialists might be
expected to benefit the most from this volume, experienced scholars
may also find material of interest—orientations or insights that
stimulate new thinking about "old" material, story analysis that gen-
erates fresh contemplation that can be used in turn to reinvigorate
the class room.

That some of this book's readers will be teachers is important, for
Hemingway deserves to be remembered not only as a cultural icon
but also, and more importantly, as one of the twentieth century's
most important writers. The man whose photographs were a mass-
media commonplace in the 1950s and whose name and image continue to be used more than ever to lend cachet to various consumer
products remains important for his contributions as a writer of modern American fiction. While I give close attention in this study to the
individual stories, I have tried to avoid pedantry and have especially
tried to steer clear of critical jousting over fine points. The fine

points are important, and such jousting can be both enjoyable and illuminating, but it should be reserved for the specialized journals. The curious student and the more experienced reader of Hemingway alike are meant to feel at home here.

I have tried to adapt my criticism to the author's work rather than jam the work into a set of a priori assumptions. Great fiction transcends such assumptions, and the writers of great fiction outlive the rule makers of any generation and moralizers of whatever stripe. While I feel free to note Hemingway's weaknesses, the book is not an extended attack, nor the sort of concerted exercise in deflation that seems to have become popular in the last twenty years. I did not set out to write a hagiography but a piece of criticism, as honest as I could make it, on an author whose work I hold in high esteem.

I have included a short biographical chapter that concentrates on those aspects of Hemingway's life that seem to me most likely to assist the reader in gaining a deeper appreciation of *In Our Time*. The reader may find that it is helpful to understand some of the larger forces shaping the writer's life, forces that necessarily have a bearing on the work. After these preliminary observations, however, I have avoided narrowly autobiographical interpretations of the sort that claim that the fishing trip in "Big Two-Hearted River" is just like Hemingway's own fishing trip in ways a, b, and c but differs in ways, x, y, and z. Many of the fictions in *In Our Time* are highly autobiographical, but what may come as a surprise to some readers is that many are not autobiographical in any important way whatsoever. As a Hemingway scholar I have delighted in reading the fine biographies that exist, but my wish here is to allow the stories to have a life of their own, independent as much as possible from that of their world-famous author. If the reader is disappointed in this critical approach, I plead the practical exigency of limited space and note that Hemingway has not been underserved by biographical studies. The biographically inclined reader is referred to the bibliography at the end of this study.

The heart of the book is the textual analysis. I operate under the assumption that the critic's first duty is to respond to the story as it exists rather than cling to a predetermined thesis. I hope that I have avoided thesis-mongering, which is perhaps the worst sort of pedantry. Nevertheless, several themes recur in the analysis: that *In Our Time* is the most experimental of all of Hemingway's texts; that the daring and boldness Hemingway brought to the work were radical — he reshaped the landscape for American fiction writers — and he himself would never recapture this experimental strain with the same vigor; that along with, perhaps even despite, this modernist strain, Hemingway retained a good many traditional values; that (contrary to the claims of some notable contemporary critics) World War I was a watershed for Hemingway and occupies a central place in *In Our Time;* and that for every Hemingway stereotype that the reader may believe he or she has found fulfilled, there will be another instance where the stereotype is obviously contradicted.

The last point would profit from further elaboration, for the Hemingway reputation is still encrusted with layer upon layer of machismo. Many people, having heard about Hemingway but never having read him, come to his works looking for a bullying patriarch. Such readers had better be prepared for some surprises. Among American writers, only Mark Twain can be said to have achieved in his own day the celebrity status Hemingway achieved in his. It is doubtful, however, that any other writer's public image is so at odds with so much of what one actually finds in his texts. The myth of the life — and, yes, what a life it was! — has proven to enhance the pleasure of reading Hemingway but also to prevent seeing what his stories actually say and do. Many misconceptions retain their currency even among people who should know better. By way of encouraging in the reader an open-mindedness and a proper attentiveness to what is actually in the stories, let me briefly address two elements of the myth: Hemingway as action hero and Hemingway as "hypermasculinist."

Despite his status as a man of action — an image that he deliberately cultivated — Hemingway's fame should not rest primarily on his reputation as an action writer. For one thing, even in the stories of high outward drama, such as "The Doctor and the Doctor's Wife," "The Battler," and "Big Two-Hearted River" in *In Our Time,* or in a later story such as "The Short, Happy Life of Francis Macomber" (1936), with its engrossing narration of hunting scenes, the external action is always a backdrop for the more important inner dramas that are being waged. Furthermore, the Hemingway canon contains many stories that have virtually no outward drama, and even some of the ostensibly "action" stories or "action" scenes are not really action-packed. From an adventurer's perspective "Big Two-Hearted River" is a yawner; and although in the later stories we find Francis Macomber running from lions and, after his change of heart, running down buffalo, we also find the moribund Harry spending all of "The Snows of Kilimanjaro" (1936) lying in his cot. Readers new to Hemingway's work but familiar with his celebrity persona often express surprise that so many of his better stories contain so little outward action and overt drama. To read Hemingway for the first time is to discover that the most important drama is unspoken, latent, submerged.

Reading Hemingway for the first time can elicit other surprises, as well. College students frequently come to the texts armed with their "knowledge" of Hemingway's tough-guy male chauvinism only to discover how often his fictions run counter to this easy stereotype. If his stories contain weak, damaged, and needy women, they also contain more than their full share of weak, damaged, and needy men. Even though Nick dumps Marjorie in "The End of Something," it is he who adopts the attitude of the wounded victim and she who remains self-possessed. For every put-upon man suffering at the hands of his wife, such as Dr. Adams, there is a callous husband or boyfriend, such as George in "Cat in the Rain" or "the young gentleman" of "Out of Season," who wounds the woman who loves him; and in no way do the stories dismiss, let alone condone, such callousness. Self-centered and self-destructive male behavior is there to be witnessed for all who will allow themselves to do so.

And so are the many "unmanly" moments in Hemingway. For every moment of masculinity triumphant, for every Villalta in his moment of tauromaquian glory, there is a battle-fatigued Nick Adams so overexcited by a fish he has hooked and then lost that he has to sit down to collect himself. This scene from "Big Two-Hearted River" reads like a modern male equivalent of the Victorian heroine overcome with the vapors. Whatever masculinized glories may exist are contingent and temporary, and Hemingway displays this fact not only in the early *In Our Time* but over and over again throughout his career. *The Sun Also Rises* (1926) depicts the triumphs of the young and vigorous Pedro Romero in the bullring, but it also gives full measure to the depiction of Belmonte, a has-been who not so long ago had been his generation's Romero, the best bullring artist of his day. *In Our Time* includes, in the story "The Battler," an even more grotesque version of the broken-down star in Ad Francis, whose days of tough-guy fame proved to be short-lived and who fell far and fast when he fell. He is damaged goods now, living on the margins of a society that once made a champion of him.

The celebration of masculinity, scenes of male bonding, machismo victorious — all of these hackneyed and unidimensional expectations of Hemingway's work must give way to the much richer, much more nuanced, much more complicated world that is actually present as early as *In Our Time*. The opening of the Hemingway archive in 1975, Scribners' publication of the highly edited *The Garden of Eden* (1986), and new modes of scholarly thinking have all helped readers to see what was really always there: a writer who wished to explore questions of gender and sexuality in a modern way. Readers who disabuse themselves of preconceptions and are willing to consider the entire Hemingway oeuvre rather than pass final judgment on the basis of selected instances culled from a particular handful of fictions may find these explorations rich and interesting or may find them disappointing. But if they are honest, they will not be able to say that Hemingway's work presents them with rigid gender definitions or stereotyped conventions of sexual behavior.

Thus, the present book opens with a caution and a plea to allow Hemingway the due earned by any serious writer: to give the text a chance, to read what has actually been written in all its fullness, complication, and even contradictoriness; and only then to judge.

Citation of Selected Letters

References to the letters of Hemingway are to *Selected Letters, 1917–1961,* edited by Carlos Baker (New York: Scribner's, 1981). The date of the letter will be given in parentheses in the form day/month/year, followed by the abbreviation *SL* and page number.

1: The Historical and Biographical Context

ERNEST HEMINGWAY WAS NOT YET NINETEEN when he arrived in Europe as a volunteer ambulance driver for the American Red Cross. After a brief stay in Paris he was sent to Italy, where he first transported wounded soldiers then volunteered as the head of a rolling canteen unit, the job he had when his leg was severely wounded by a shell explosion. By the summer of 1918 the Great War was nearing its end, but not before providing a young man from suburban Chicago with some rapid lessons in growing up modern. Although his war experience was brief, Hemingway was changed by the conflict in ways both predictable and subtle. His first assignment was to retrieve the body parts of men and women who were victims of a munitions plant explosion near Milan, an experience he would later use in "A Natural History of the Dead (1932)." Like millions of his generation, he saw at first hand the futile destruction of World War I, the catastrophe that swept away the nineteenth century once and for all. As shocking as his war experiences were, and as anxious as his wounds undoubtedly made him, he did not feel the full import of his injury immediately. Nor did he immediately understand the broader implications of the changes brought about by the war. A more profound emotional response and a fuller understanding of the war's ramifications, both personal and societal, developed steadily over the years between his return to the United States and the publication in 1925 of *In Our Time,* whose vignettes and stories are infused with postwar disaffection and anomie.

As with tens of thousands of his generation, Hemingway's wounding brought with it a hero's status — but also intimations of mortality just at the stage of life, the transition years of late adolescence and young adulthood, when most people feel invulnerable. Moreover, he had fallen in love with his nurse, Agnes von Kurowsky, while convalescing in a Milan hospital, and they had talked of marriage. Shortly after returning home Hemingway received a Dear

John letter from Kurowsky and learned the shock and the quality of pain brought by *that* sort of wound. She was his first love; but for the adventurous and vivacious Agnes (who was eight years his senior), Hemingway was an attractive and special friend for whom she rather quickly lost romantic feelings once he was no longer a part of her daily life.[1] Not yet two years out of high school, Hemingway had been introduced to modern forms of suffering and chaos and also to the age-old anguish of loss and disappointment. One of his greatest gifts, which he displayed even as a young writer, was the ability to blend the new and specifically modern with the abiding and recurrent elements of human experience.

Dr. Clarence Edmonds Hemingway practiced family and obstetrical medicine in the Chicago suburb of Oak Park, where Ernest Miller Hemingway, the second of six children, was born on 21 July 1899. His father's love of the outdoors, of hunting and fishing and woodsman's skills, would quickly take root in young Ernest. Before he was two months old, he made the first of many summer journeys to northern Michigan, where his parents built a cottage on Bear (later called Walloon) Lake. As a boy, Ernest spent every summer there, and the small towns and countryside of the region would become the setting of several Nick Adams stories in *In Our Time*. The rest of the year the family lived in a large house on Kenilworth Avenue in Oak Park that Hemingway's mother, Grace Hall Hemingway, had planned. His father's practice prospered, and his mother commanded a handsome hourly rate for giving voice lessons. From her Hemingway inherited his artistic inclinations, and it was, no doubt, at her urging that he began to develop them — though he would attain to a much more twentieth-century sensibility than the essentially Victorian Grace ever cultivated.

The Oak Park of Hemingway's day retained its suburban, separate-from-Chicago character. Its north side, where the Hemingways lived, was a white, Protestant, upper-middle-class community, progressively Republican in politics, conservative if not restrictive in its

---

[1] Henry S. Villard and James Nagel provide the fullest account of the relationship between Hemingway and Kurowsky in their *Hemingway in Love and War* (1989).

social mores, peopled largely by college-educated professionals and businessmen who saw to it that the school system remained strong.[2] Hemingway's outdoor summers and solid upbringing, however, were accompanied by personal and family problems. There is abundant evidence that Ernest, like his father and other members of his family, suffered from depression, which became more severe as he matured but manifested itself incipiently in his childhood. He seems to have been subject early on to spells of black foreboding of death and to have become fearful in the night. Much of his juvenilia, including stories that he published in his high-school literary magazine, gives evidence of a preoccupation with the violent and the morbid.

The family problems became more severe as Hemingway grew up. As he got older he increasingly expressed resentment both of his mother's smothering pieties and, even more, of what he saw as her domination of his father, whom Hemingway came to consider dangerously weak. This familial discord works its way into several Nick Adams stories, perhaps most notably "The Doctor and the Doctor's Wife," and is part of the creative context for several stories in *In Our Time*. His father's chronic depression would lead to suicide when Hemingway was twenty-nine.

Hemingway was a good student in a superior high school. He participated in a large number of extracurricular activities, including the school paper and literary magazine. Despite his love of athletics and his later boasting about his boyhood prowess in various sports, the truth is that he was athletically mediocre except in hunting and fishing. After high school he disappointed his parents by deciding not to attend his father's alma mater, Oberlin College. He was eager to get out into the world and begin working as a writer, and his uncle's influence enabled him to join the *Kansas City Star* as a cub reporter. He began his writing career on the police and hospital beat, developing a style that was strongly shaped by the newspaper's 110 rules for writing. When he became famous, Hemingway expressed gratitude for the early discipline that forced him to produce terse

[2] Michael Reynolds gives an excellent description of Hemingway's Oak Park in *The Young Hemingway* (1986).

prose shorn of clichés, empty adjectives, florid rhetoric, and other forms of verbal inflation.[3]

When the United States entered World War I, Hemingway was too young for military service; in any event, he would surely have been turned down because of weak vision in his left eye. Moreover, Hemingway's father had opposed Ernest's desire to join the military after high school, though he did not try to prevent his son from volunteering for the American Red Cross a year later, in the spring of 1918. Hemingway spent eight months in Europe, much of it convalescing from his wounds and a subsequent case of jaundice. When he returned to Oak Park in 1919, he found, like many men coming back from the war, that being the victorious hero gained one, at most, only a brief moment in the sun; and Hemingway was willing to buy his moment at the expense of telling obvious stretchers about his ordeals. As Harold Krebs, his fictional alter ego in "Soldier's Home," finds out, there was little from the war experiences that would be of use in building an ordinary life.

After his long convalescence, and after being precipitously dumped by Agnes von Kurowsky, Hemingway was much more keenly aware of the fragility of things. He was subject to black moods, and for a long time he could not sleep without a light. His parents worried, as do Harold Krebs's, that he was content to drift aimlessly through the first years of adulthood. The war and his first taste of foreign travel had given him experience and confidence and a desire to seek further adventure but had also affected him in a darker, more troubling fashion. He was not jaded, but he was aware that the lessons he had learned as a youngster could not provide a shield against certain kinds of vulnerability. The men and women of his generation were susceptible to the pains and turmoil to which men and women have always been susceptible, but there were also new problems to contend with. The modern world presented forces that people had little hope of comprehending, much less overcoming. The leviathan war had amply demonstrated that, although it

---

[3] Charles A. Fenton's *The Apprenticeship of Ernest Hemingway* (1954), one of the first scholarly studies, remains a fine summary of Hemingway's experiences at the *Star*.

took several years of development and a move to Paris for Hemingway to come to a mature reckoning of the war's impact. When he first returned home, it was simply easier and more honest to go fishing in the northern woods of his youth than to try to fulfill his parents' expectations or to meet the larger world head on.

The American poet Ezra Pound, who later became Hemingway's friend, wrote in "Hugh Selwyn Mauberly" (1920) that World War I occasioned "wastage as never before" and "disillusions as never told in the old days." The scale of destruction wrought by the war had been unimaginable theretofore: ten million soldiers died; millions more were wounded; before the war finally ground to a close, yet more millions had begun to die in the Spanish influenza pandemic of 1918–1919. The boundaries between civilian and soldier had become blurred and, in many instances, had crumbled away as the eternally stalemated conflict stretched from the Straits of Dover to Switzerland, extended into Italy and the Middle East, and caused every segment of European and, eventually, American society to be mobilized in support of the "war effort." Well over 100 billion dollars was spent, and the magnitude of destruction and loss of property had no parallel. Afterward, people came to see that "the war to end all wars" had accomplished none of the goals that were trumpeted at its outset. Ultimately, it became clear that the ill-conceived Versailles Treaty that ended the First World War was nothing less than the official prelude to the next worldwide exercise in destruction.

In Europe a generation of young men had been devastated. Many of those who survived the trenches were disillusioned and bitter, and they encountered difficulties in reintegrating themselves into ordinary, workaday society. But those who had fought in the war were not alone in feeling displaced. A large segment of the younger generation was disaffected, and this mood surpassed the ordinary rebelliousness of youth both in intensity and in its impact on the whole culture. The German philosopher Oswald Spengler's despairing Nietzschean treatise *The Decline of the West* (1918; revised, 1923) struck a chord not just in his native country but throughout Europe. The gloom, despondency, and doubt were accompanied in many countries by economic crises and political instability. The losers — especially the Germans — simmered in bitterness, and the victors soon wondered what, exactly, they had won. Smaller conflicts flared up in the immediate postwar years, such as the Greco-Turkish war, which Hemingway covered as a correspondent. This is the European milieu in which Hemingway moved as a reporter, expatriate, and apprentice fiction writer. Even though there are only five paragraphs in *In Our Time* with a First World War setting, the book is infused with the war and its aftermath.

It is also infused with the historical particulars and the feel of an era lost to readers today. The book, of course, reflects the years of Hemingway's growing up, roughly 1910 to 1925, a time that has grown vague — that has long ceased to represent "our time." For example, the baseball talk in "The Three-Day Blow," with its allusions to cheating incidents and untrustworthy players, was fresher to Hemingway's contemporaries than to us. It is meant to add an edge of cynicism to the boys' essentially juvenile conversation. But while the topical quality of the volume is present in the stories, with their allusions to such matters as baseball players, veterans returning from the Rhineland, and expatriate Americans living in postwar Europe on the cheap, it comes out most strongly in the vignettes. As if to emphasize this contemporary quality, when the vignettes were published together as *in our time* in 1924, the dust jacket took the then-novel form of a collage that included a map and excerpts from newspaper articles in various languages.

While images of the Roaring Twenties still occupy a lively space in the American cultural imagination, the mainstream temper in the United States was actually quite conservative, seeking for isolation and "normalcy" after the war. The war years had introduced unprecedented repression and censorship into American civil life, and, despite the flappers and the necking in rumble seats, postwar society proved resistant to political reform and meaningful social innovation. Anti-immigrant feeling ran high in the 1920s, as did fear of Bolshevism. Doing his utmost to maintain quietude, even at the expense of breaching civil liberties, President Woodrow Wilson's attorney general, A. Mitchell Palmer, "The Fighting Quaker," aggressively deported radical immigrants and laid legally dubious injunctions on strikers and labor agitators without hesitation. The Red scares of the postwar years coincided with a rapid rise in the membership of the

Ku Klux Klan. "I can tell Wops a mile off," says policeman Boyle in "Chapter VIII" of *In Our Time,* apparently confident that he will not be reprimanded for hastily shooting a suspect dead as long as the man is a swarthy immigrant. Boyle's belligerence is matched by his ignorance: the suspect was actually Hungarian (79).

Alcoholic beverages became illegal with the enactment of the Volstead Act in 1919, so naturally for millions of people the selling, buying, and drinking of alcohol became more fascinating than ever, ensuring that bootlegging gangsters would become America's nouveau riche. Other gangsters, like Sam Cardinella in "Chapter XV" of *In Our Time,* worked at the newly organized, extremely violent extortion schemes called racketeering. The world was also full of legal violence that made just as little sense and was just as horrible as the illegal varieties that received sensationalized treatment in the press. Hemingway's readers in 1925 would remember — if not in detail, at least in general — the Greco-Turkish war of 1919–1922 that is central to three vignettes and one story in *In Our Time.* And the recent Russian Revolution and the other attempted revolutions that it spawned would have made the title character in Hemingway's "The Revolutionist" historically more immediate to his initial readers than he is to us. Still, readers then as now had to contend with the lack of political and historical background in the vignettes, short sketches that begin *in medias res* and concentrate on developing images and single events to achieve an intensity of effect. As we shall see, Hemingway was experimenting with the idea that purposely leaving out background would make his stories stronger.

The urbanization of America was already well along, and the wealthy country's material progress, while it was a wonder of the world, exacted a spiritual price and produced yearning and disgruntlement in some — especially the young. Greenwich Village became the bohemian center of America, but many artists and writers took advantage of the weakness of Continental currencies and sought a freer and more cosmopolitan life in European cities. Among these, —Paris was the strongest magnet — especially the area around Montparnasse, known as the Latin Quarter. There the artistic and literary scene merged with café life, and serious artists lived a bohemian existence in close company with poseurs, dilettantes, wastrels, and dropouts of various stripes.

At the urging of Sherwood Anderson, who was by then a celebrated author, the newlywed Hemingway and his wife Hadley (née Richardson) whom he had met during a brief sojourn in Chicago, sailed for Paris in December 1921, with Hemingway's sights firmly set on the writing life. In Paris he would meet Pound, Gertrude Stein, Ford Madox Ford, James Joyce, F. Scott Fitzgerald, Robert McAlmon, and others who would play a formative role in his apprentice years. Prior to his arrival, Paris had already become established as a cosmopolitan center of the literary and artistic avant-garde. By choosing Paris as his expatriate headquarters Hemingway was able to submerge himself in a heady literary and artistic milieu, and he made the most of his opportunities. With no literary achievements to recommend him but with a strong and attractive personality and an obvious enthusiasm for the writing life, within a year he would befriend several key modernist figures and be fully involved in the Parisian literary circle.

Furnished with letters of recommendation from the kindly Anderson, Hemingway soon met Stein and Pound, the two writers who exerted the most direct influence on his development. Stein's home was part modernist art gallery and part salon where many of modernism's brighter stars could be seen shining. Although he had some experience of modern painting from his visits to the Art Institute of Chicago, Hemingway was relatively unschooled in modern art. Stein began his immersion in it. She and her brother Leo had always shared a quick eye for important developments in the visual arts, and on her walls hung works by Paul Cézanne, Pablo Picasso, Henri Matisse, and other modernist giants then considered avant-garde. For his part, Pound treated Hemingway as a promising writer worthy of tutelage and pointed out significant modern authors that he should read. Sylvia Beach, whose bookstore, Shakespeare and Company, was an important center of Parisian literary life, provided the library needed by the student writer. It was Beach who first published Joyce's modernist opus *Ulysses* (1922), and she promoted young writers by stocking their books, providing encouragement, and instituting an affordable lending policy of which Hemingway took advantage for his autodidactic course in world literature.

Before his departure for Paris, Hemingway had secured an agreement from the *Toronto Star* to give him occasional assignments and to accept unsolicited articles, but he had wider ambitions. His journalistic work kept him writing and was a welcome source of income. The traveling it occasioned contributed immensely to Hemingway's growing understanding of his time, thrusting him into direct contact with major political and military events of the day. His experiences as a correspondent also provided him with a good bit of material on which he honed his literary skills, material that eventually found its way into the collection of vignettes he collected in the small chapbook *in our time* in 1924 and republished in *In Our Time*, where he called them "chapters."

It would be difficult to overstate how different life in the Latin Quarter was from the Oak Park milieu of Hemingway's upbringing. People lived their lives and discussed and practiced their art with an aggressive sense of freedom and a fervor for experimentation. Drink, drugs, and experiments in sexual variety and gender roles were as much a part of the scene as the unrestrained and plentiful talk about art and literature. The young Hemingway felt the need to break free from familial and societal constraints; thus, he sought to be a part of what the Latin Quarter represented. Yet, part of him always remained aloof from what he saw there. He put great stock in working and hoped to set himself above the many dilettantes and phonies who idled away their time and only talked a great artistic game. He yearned to achieve something more lasting than those who may have gained commercial success but wrote second-rate books. While not primarily a satirical writer, Hemingway quickly came to cast a skeptical eye on much of what transpired in the Quarter, and he saw that Paris was largely what one was willing and able to make of it. As an older man writing his fictionalized memoirs, he looked back at these apprentice years in Paris and referred to the city as "a moveable feast." Hemingway became a man of serial favorite places and of special locations that made him feel alive. But Paris was the most important of them all. In this inexpensive, free-living, cosmopolitan capital of the arts, a hopeful young man from suburban Illinois forged one of the most distinctive voices in modern literature.

2: *In Our Time* as Modernist Literature: Placing the Text in the Literary Landscape

Hemingway's words strike you, each one, as if they were pebbles fetched fresh from a brook. They live and shine, each in its place. So one of his pages has the effect of a brook-bottom into which you look down through flowing water. The words form a tesellation, each in order beside the other.

— Ford Madox Ford[1]

AN APPRECIATION OF *In Our Time* had best begin with a discussion of literary technique, for Hemingway's literary durability depends primarily upon the style and methods he developed as a young man in Paris, as does his status as a modernist writer. More than the action of his stories, more than his characters, it is the way the characters and the action are presented that matters. It is fair to say that the very ethos of the stories — their mood, tone, and worldview — could not exist except as they are embodied in Hemingway's style. The way of his words conducts us toward the tragic stoicism that underlies the volume and continued to receive expression in the best of his succeeding work. Indeed, it is nearer the mark to say that without the style and method the tragic stoicism cannot come into full being. The worldview and the style are inseparable. His technique has won Hemingway many readers who do not hunt or fish, who have never camped, who find bullfighting barbaric, who would never hop aboard a freight train, and who find whoring in taxicabs or "potting" enemy soldiers unimaginable. Most interesting of all is the way Hemingway's simplified verbal style is embodied in the complex, cubist structure of *In Our Time*. Simultaneously with the development of his prose style Hemingway worked on refining his

---

[1] Quoted from Edmund Wilson, "Hemingway: Gauge of Morale" (18).

"craft of omission,"[2] a combination of techniques whose ultimate achievement was to intensify the suggestive powers of his stories. His surfaces are vivid and sensually rich, satisfying the traditional demand that fiction provide a concrete representation of the world; but the stories also contain elusive and ambiguous depths, depths that retain their elusiveness and ambiguity because they rely on suggestion rather than on elaboration.

Ernest Hemingway had work to do when he arrived in Paris. He did not get off the ship with a fully developed conception of modern writing, nor did he see precisely how he would make his mark in it. Hemingway's American juvenilia show a young man hoping to make a living as a writer of popular magazine fiction. He did arrive in Paris possessing the fundamentals of what would become his style in *In Our Time*, but the fundamentals needed further refinement, and he needed to rid himself of the derivative and formulaic approach to fiction that marks his commercially oriented juvenilia. Furthermore, his writing needed to be harnessed to a more mature and specifically modern postwar vision of the world. *In Our Time* is the culmination of Hemingway's literary apprenticeship in Paris, a time when he had nothing to lose professionally. It remains the most insistently experimental of all his books because it is the product of the one period of his life when he participated intently in a literary scene, and the temper of that milieu was distinctly modernist. In later years Hemingway would withdraw from literary scenes and cut off his literary friendships, choosing to live a life given over by turns to action, to travel, and to artistic isolation among non-writer cronies. But in his early twenties he consciously strove to take part in the modernist movement. One can acknowledge the nostalgia and self-serving that are apt to function in memoirs and still believe the Hemingway of *A Moveable Feast* (1964) when he testifies that the expatriate 1920s were glorious years of self-creation.

Hemingway wanted not just to become famous in his time but to develop his craft to such a degree that his work would endure as true art endures. In a word, his ambition was to become the best. In later

---

[2] Susan F. Beegel uses this phrase as a part of the title for her 1988 study *Hemingway's Craft of Omission*.

years he would boast that a literary career was like a series of boxing matches and that he had knocked out all of his adversaries except Leo Tolstoy and William Shakespeare, but in his early twenties success seemed to him slow in coming. From a more dispassionate vantage point one can see how quickly he managed first to make a name for himself with other writers and then to put a distinctive and indelible imprint on American letters. His talent and discipline for work gained him notoriety within expatriate literary circles, and before the end of the decade he would garner international acclaim.

Any present-day difficulties in identifying the importance of Hemingway's influence can be attributed to the fact that he has been subsumed into the literary culture. Rather than being seen as an imposing or, at least, prominent feature on the literary landscape, his work is subject to being taken by uninformed contemporary readers as "natural," as the way good fiction writers write. If the lay of the verbal landscape has been re-engineered for over seven decades, the chief engineer may be forgotten, and the re-engineering will be hard to discern, no matter how radical it was to begin with — and it *was* radical. Until he became connected with important members of the avant-garde literary set, Hemingway could find no place for the stories and poems he was writing in Paris. He was ready to write for his time, but his time was not ready for him.

One useful way of conceiving Hemingway's achievement is to place it in the context of nineteenth-century realism. Henry James, the most accomplished American stylist of his generation, had likened effective literary prose to a windowpane onto the world. Although he took no interest in theorizing about the issue, Hemingway shared a belief common among modernist writers that good fiction transcended being a mere transcription of the world and thus achieved a status that was truer than true. Comparing his journalism with his efforts to forge a lasting literary style, Hemingway said in *Death in the Afternoon* (1932):

> In writing for a newspaper you told what happened on that day; but the real thing, the sequence of motion and fact which made the emotion and which would be as valid in a year or in ten years or, with luck and if you stated it purely enough, always, was beyond me and I was working very hard to try to get it (2).

Hemingway's work "to get it" seemed so promising to Pound that he included the young writer as one of six authors in the series "Inquest into the State of Contemporary English Prose," even though Hemingway's literary production at that point was slender, to say the least.

For Hemingway, as for other modernist artists and writers, new times required the development of new techniques. "Make it new" was Pound's pithy manifesto for modernists, and while Hemingway's fictions are less radically experimental than those of such contemporaries as Joyce or William Faulkner or Virginia Woolf, he, too, broke with convention and determined to forge a distinctive modern style. As a nineteen-year-old home from the war Hemingway had read little modern literature.[3] His earliest ambition was to concoct the sort of slick story that would sell to large-circulation magazines such as *The Saturday Evening Post*. Fortunately, his early attempts at commercially oriented freelancing met with the usual rejections; and even more luckily, in 1921, while living in Chicago and working for a small corporate monthly magazine, he met Anderson, read his *Winesburg, Ohio* (1919) and listened to the eminent author's advice on living and working as a serious writer. Anderson told him to read D. H. Lawrence, the great nineteenth-century Russians (of whom Ivan Turgenev would become young Hemingway's favorite), and Stein. Anderson's stories showed American writers that they need not dedicate their art to the dense accumulation of surface features, nor to expounding social structures in minute detail, nor — least of all — to the construction of well-made plots and catchy endings. Anderson instead took as his aim the examination of half-realized motives and thwarted emotions that remained poorly understood both by the characters who experienced these feelings and also, usually, by those around them. His accomplishment was outstripped by the best writers of the succeeding generation, but he left an important legacy to Hemingway and others in his lyricism and in his wish

---

[3] Although Oak Park's high school provided a fine education in Hemingway's time, the literature curriculum would not have included contemporary writers. Indeed, few American writers of any era were read there, as the English tradition was thought to be more important.

to probe beneath the psyche's surface even in the seemingly simplest of characters.

Anderson himself had been influenced and championed by Stein, whom Hemingway would meet the following year in Paris. On her first visit to Hemingway's apartment, Stein, who professed admiration for Gustave Flaubert's verbal precision, read some of his work and urged him to "begin over again and concentrate" (Stein 213). In particular, Hemingway came to see how Stein used repetition to achieve rhythmic and subliminal effects; one can observe his deliberate incorporation of repetition in several stories in *In Our Time*, most insistently in "Soldier's Home" and more subtly in many other passages. Stein's predilection for short words also rubbed off on Hemingway, but the surface similarities between their two styles actually mask a more important fundamental difference: Hemingway learned to use language in a double way. Stein's essential subject became language itself, which she played with as the raw material of her fiction. Although Hemingway also prided himself on being a craftsman with words, and although the attentive reader will discern the deliberate stylization behind the apparently simple sentences (Hemingway quickly becomes mannered when his style fails him), it is experience, life itself, character and incident, that furnish his basic material. Stein used her simple diction and syntactical experiments to form fictional wholes that were complex to the point of incomprehensibility; Hemingway's language is always lucid, grounded, and sensual, and his narratives retain a forward drive that is often absent in Stein's.

Although Hemingway always had his antennae up to detect poseurs, and although something in his Midwestern makeup made him distrust artsy salon affairs, at Stein's house he was able to familiarize himself with the work of cutting-edge artists. Some critics have maintained that Hemingway was actually little influenced by the paintings of Cézanne, Picasso, and others that hung on the walls at Stein's apartment and about which Stein undoubtedly held forth. But while he was working on "Big Two-Hearted River," Hemingway wrote to Stein that he was deliberately attempting to achieve in words the effects Cézanne did on canvas. Working in this vein was exacting, he declared, but he also implied that when one got it right, it was worth it (15/8/1924: *SL* 122). This letter should be taken as more than the ingratiating effort of a young disciple. It is that, of course, but it is also a sincere early expression of Hemingway's artistic aims. I will discuss later his attempts to translate Cézanne's techniques from painting to writing, but for now it should be noted that the letter reveals Hemingway's desire to achieve fictional modernity through the perfection of style. The letter is written from the conviction that the writer must not content himself with being a mere spinner of yarns but, no less than the painter, must be a hardworking craftsman intent on refining his art.

Shortly after publishing *In Our Time* Hemingway wrote an extended parody of Anderson, *Torrents of Spring* (1926), and eventually he and Stein turned on each other. But he always remained loyal to Pound, the third important benefactor of his early days. Besides fashioning his own poetic career, Pound generously made himself instrumental in advancing the work of several important modernist writers. He set a reading agenda for Hemingway, proposing those modern authors who had not been a part of the tradition-bound curriculum at Oak Park High School. And he characteristically threw himself into securing publishers for Hemingway, who later said that Pound gave him the most practical, concrete advice on writing that anyone ever had. Undoubtedly Pound, the imagist poet, advised Hemingway to focus on the visual and to trim away excess verbage. "ANYTHING put on top of the subject is BAD," Pound wrote Hemingway in his typical faux-hillbilly epistolary persona. "Licher-chure is mostly blanketing up a subject. Too much MAKINGS. The subject is always interesting enough without the blankets." Pound also urged him to get into his stories quickly, not to put "two [*sic*] much mat between the frame and the picture."[4] Wisely, Hemingway did not always cut passages that Pound may have found too "licherary," as one can see, for example, in the moving and meaningful opening of "The End of Something."

The relationship worked because Pound enjoyed playing the teacher, because Hemingway was still capable of accepting criticism

---

[4] Both quotations are from a 21 December 1926 letter to Hemingway (John Fitzgerald Kennedy Library collection, Boston).

as a young writer, because the men shared a commitment to technique and a will to style, and, probably, because Pound was a poet and Hemingway a fiction writer. At most, any rivalry between them would be indirect. In any case, Pound was giving Hemingway advice that he was quite prepared to hear and was, indeed, already practicing after a fashion. For one thing, the *Kansas City Star* had preached directness of expression and economy of diction in its house style sheet. Then, in his journalistic dispatches from Europe to North America, Hemingway had become skilled in the art of "cablese." Intercontinental communication by telegraph put a premium on brevity chiefly for financial reasons: journalists sending fewer words saved their publishers money since telegraph companies charged by the word. Cablese demanded that its practitioner, like an imagist poet, select only the most telling detail for inclusion in his report.

Journalistic training and necessity, then, merged with the writer's predilections to create a style that was, in many respects, poetic. In several letters written during the 1940s the eminent poet Wallace Stevens elaborated his admiration for Hemingway's capacity to depict "extraordinary reality" without any false steps toward mere sensationalism (Stevens 412). Asked whom he would recommend for a Princeton University lecture series on poetry, Stevens proposed Hemingway, whose entire career (with the exception of a few early little-magazine poems) had been built on prose fiction! "Most people don't think of Hemingway as a poet, but obviously he is a poet," Stevens wrote, "and I should say, offhand, the most significant of living poets" (411). Stevens had in mind Hemingway's ability to infuse a scene with emotion, to cut to the core of a character, to reveal that character in a moment of stress and to impress that scene indelibly on the mind's eye of his readers — all with an extraordinary economy. Hemingway's writing is condensed as good poetry is condensed, and one key to the poetic compression of Hemingway's prose is his use of images. In a landmark article on Hemingway's style, Harry Levin observes: "By presenting a succession of images, each of which has its brief moment when it commands the reader's undivided attention, [Hemingway] achieves his special vividness and fluidity" (78). Levin's remark applies not only to the full-fledged short stories, where — in "Big Two-Hearted River," for example — trout, tree lines, grasshoppers, tent pegs, sizzling grease, fishing lines, object after object alternately serves as the focus of acute attention; the remark also applies to the vignettes of *In Our Time,* which can be viewed as intense examples of prose that achieves the provocative economy of form and rich suggestiveness typical of poetry. The selection of successive images is key in the development of any number of the vignettes. Michael Reynolds has gone so far as to say that the vignettes as they originally appeared together in *in our time* "were more like Eliot's *Waste Land* than any recognizable prose model" ("Hemingway's *In Our Time:* The Biography of a Book" 39).[5]

Thus Hemingway helped to break down the barriers between poetry and prose, genre-bending itself being another hallmark accomplishment of the modernist writers. The tendency to prosify poetry is at least as old as William Wordsworth, who declared that poetry ought to be written in "a selection of language really used by men," that is, a language traditionally thought more suitable for prose or nonliterary writing. But the poeticizing of prose was never accomplished so fully as it has been in the twentieth century. Hemingway's poetic bent is remarkable, though, not only for its novelty but also for its insistent inclusion of American vernacular. In "Chapter IX" of *In Our Time* we read:

> He couldn't hardly lift his arm. He tried five times and the crowd was quiet because it was a good bull and it looked like him or the bull and then he finally made it. He sat down in the sand and puked and they held a cape over him while the crowd hollered and threw things down into the bull ring. (83)

"Couldn't hardly," "it looked like him or the bull," "puked," "hollered" — all these locutions carry a particularly American demotic flavor, even though they are being applied to a quintessentially Spanish subject. Hemingway's declaration in *Green Hills of Africa*

---

[5] In her study of Hemingway, Wendolyn Tetlow concentrates on elaborating the poetic nature of *In Our Time,* likening the book to the modern poetic sequence.

(1935) that modern American literature flows out of Mark Twain's *Adventures of Huckleberry Finn* (1884) indicates his determination to work in the vernacular strain of American fiction. He had striven assiduously to weed out fine writing, superfluous narratorial commentary, and rhetorical adornment. The First World War plays a pivotal role here, for it helped to provoke an artistic change right at the baseline level of literary diction. The war had been built on a sort of rhetoric that now rang utterly false. Harold Krebs is nauseated in "Soldier's Home" by his mother's treacly nineteenth-century pieties. Her world is no longer "the" world, and the very language she uses has been rendered worthless by the war. In a famous passage in *A Farewell to Arms*, Frederic Henry feels embarrassment, even moral outrage when he hears "abstract words such as glory, honor, courage, or hallow" (185). Hemingway's skeptical care not to use cheapened and worn-out words was already evident as he created the fictions of *In Our Time*. Pound's "licherchure" is banished in favor of the authentic voices of the age.

This authenticity is to be found both in Hemingway's narrative voices and in his dialogue. The dialogue created a sensation in its own day and retains its vivid life on the page three-quarters of a century later, when its *Smart-Set* hipness has long since faded. Like other aspects of his best writing, the dialogue tends to be spare, shorn of philosophizing and abstractions, and given to understatement. And it is frequently presented directly by the narrator without interruption or tag lines, as if it were a transcript. It is at once natural and yet highly stylized, full of implications and submerged energies that the reader senses lie ready to burst onto the page at some crisis point in the story. "I'm going down and get that kitty," declares the young wife early in "Cat in the Rain," the entirety of her unhappy heart loaded into that short statement. And thus it is with the simple but sharp exchanges between Nick and Marjorie in "The End of Something" or Tiny and the young gentleman in "Out of Season." The words spoken point toward, but carry no explanation of, the problems that beset these couples, making the dialogue a key feature of Hemingway's great art of implication.

Although Hemingway's prose may seem merely simple, it is much more accurate to think of it — like much modern painting —

as deliberately *simplified*. At the level of the sentence Hemingway's early prose is lean and burnished. In the poem "Years of the Dog" the American poet Archibald MacLeish likened the young Hemingway to a craftsman in wood, declaring that he "Whittled a style for his time from a walnut stick / In a carpenter's loft in a street of that April city" (377). The hardness and durability of walnut make MacLeish's metaphor an apt one, and one that must have pleased Hemingway. The Hemingway of *In Our Time* put a premium on directness and authenticity, emphasizing nouns and verbs, using adjectives and adverbs sparingly. It should be acknowledged here that Hemingway's style changed over the years; indeed, his efforts, even as an established writer, to change and develop have seldom been appreciated. Nevertheless, simple sentence constructions are a central feature of his early style. Hemingway's goal in cultivating his particular combination of concreteness and simplicity was to create a prose alive with emotion. In *Death in the Afternoon* he describes his biggest challenge as a young writer: "aside from knowing truly what you really felt, rather than what you were supposed to feel, and had been taught to feel, it [the challenge] was to put down what really happened in action; what the actual things were which produced the emotion that you experienced" (2).[6] Likewise, attempting to explain his goals in *In Our Time* to his father, whom he knew to be disturbed by his work, Hemingway wrote: "You see I'm trying in all my stories to get the feeling of the actual life across — not just to depict life — or criticize it — but to actually make it alive. So that when you read something by me you actually experience the thing" (20/3/1925: *SL* 153).

In his efforts to create writing he hoped would enable his readers to "actually experience the thing," Hemingway joined other modernist writers and artists in smashing the underpinnings of nineteenth-century realism, which seemed to say that accurately representing the world was equivalent to telling the truth. While the surface components of Hemingway's stories are vivid and believable and do fulfill

---

[6] Carlos Baker and Hugh Kenner have discussed the similarities between Hemingway's aesthetic hopes and T. S. Eliot's famous formulation of the objective correlative (Baker, *Writer as Artist* 54–57; Kenner 151–152).

Henry James's prescription for transparent writing, Elizabeth Dewberry Vaughn is correct in arguing that ultimately Hemingway's work is less concerned with representational accuracy for its own sake than it is with creating "forms of representation that require interpretation" (3). If realism refined to its highest pitch (as practiced by James, for example) had sought to conceal its artifice, if it had sought to be utterly illusionistic, Hemingway's writing presents us with a brilliant paradox. For he is a masterful scene painter, and, at the same time, like a modernist painter, he creates a whole that ineluctably reminds the intelligent reader that fiction is fiction, not life; it is an artificial, fabricated thing.

This is not to make of Hemingway an early metafictionist, someone whose primary interest in writing fictions is to belabor the question of their ontological status. Such an abstract, self-referential conception of fiction would have bored him. Nor did he pursue the notion that fiction writing is no more than high-level verbal game-playing, endlessly folding back on itself and other texts and losing sight of the world. He did, however, explore the status of the writer and the nature of writing, and he did so with a greater intensity as he grew older. For one thing, many of his protagonists are writers, including Nick Adams. But in *In Our Time* Nick's status as a writer is only hinted at in "Big Two-Hearted River," and Hemingway never made any subsequent efforts to explore it in an extended way.[7] Neither a postmodern metafictionist nor a nineteenth-century realist,

---

[7] For the most strenuous argument for Hemingway as metafictionist, see Debra Moddlemog's article listed in the bibliography. In a long passage deleted from the end of the story at Stein's urging, Hemingway had explored Nick's thoughts about writing at considerable length and had even revealed that Nick had written "Indian Camp" (and so, presumably, the rest of the volume, as well). But the fact remains that Hemingway chose not to include this section in the published version of the story — nor did he ever restore it, work it into a new story, or create a new version of Nick as writer. All we know about Nick as a writer in "Big Two-Hearted River" is that part of his distress, part of what he needs to "leave behind," is "the need to write" (134).

Hemingway resides in the company of his contemporary experimental writers, creating, like them, new demands on his readers.[8]

These demands arise, above all, because Hemingway dedicated himself to the art of indirection and implication. "Unwritten stories" was what he initially called the series of sketches that — in a somewhat long and quite indirect manner — came to form part of *In Our Time*. He compared good fiction to an iceberg: "I always try to write on the principle of the iceberg. There is seven-eighths of it underwater for every part that shows. Anything you know you can eliminate and it only strengthens your iceberg. It is the part that doesn't show" (quoted in Meyers 139). This indirection was often achieved by withholding certain traditional functions from his narrator and, thus, information from his readers. Hemingway shared in the modernist tendency to create storytelling personae who avoid obtruding overt judgments. Action, image, and dialogue are presented with little or no narratorial commentary that would tip the author's hand. Humphrey Carpenter has described Hemingway as writing "anti-narratives deliberately deprived of 'signs' to the reader of an event's dramatic importance or its significance" (178).[9]

Such dramatically presented narratives place demands on the reader that nineteenth-century fiction typically does not. The reader's powers of inference are strenuously exercised, and he or she is repeatedly called upon to collaborate with the author in producing

---

[8] Early versions of Hemingway as a literary naif or a "dumb ox" who luckily produced marvelous stories in spite of himself were never correct, though they tenaciously clung to Hemingway once they had been uttered. Although it has not always been so among critics, the depth of Hemingway's literary intelligence and his wide reading are now taken for granted by Hemingway scholars. One finds, however, that this aspect of Hemingway is far from universal knowledge in the general reading public, despite recent biographers' attempts to enlarge on it. Michael Reynolds has done the most extensive work in suggesting the depths and dimensions of Hemingway's literary self-education, beginning with his *Hemingway's Reading*.

[9] Wayne C. Booth has produced a useful and detailed consideration of "showing vs. telling" in his *The Rhetoric of Fiction*.

meaning. Reading requires a new sort of patience and attentiveness, a willingness to suspend the desire for missing information until a later point in the story (or forever). The reader must get rid of the wish for the author's strong hand guiding him or her to formulate indubitably correct judgments. The payoff comes in the rich ambiguities of the stories and in the emotional resonance produced by Hemingway's craft of omission. As he explained: "you could omit anything if you knew that you omitted and the omitted part would strengthen the story and make people feel something more than they understood" (*A Moveable Feast* 75). Again, the author stresses feeling, and the narrative implications are obvious: the reader will have detective work to do. Thus, Hemingway's stories often embody moral tendencies, but they avoid indulging in authorial moralizing.

Finally, consistent with his technical innovations and with his desire to develop the vernacular tradition, Hemingway joined other modern writers intent on stretching the definition of what constitutes a fit subject for literature. Although he was interested in shock value for something besides its own sake (he thought the dadaists silly, for example), the young man brought up in suburban Oak Park was intent on conveying the new, tough realities of the postwar world; and if his audience was shocked from its complacency and forced to confront its limited views of the world, then one part of his job had been done. The fight to make high art out of supposedly low subjects and to examine previously taboo themes had already been going on for several decades, but the postwar generation of artists and writers felt — with some notable exceptions — an acute desire to sweep away the remnants of Victorian taboos and hypocrisies that still clung tenaciously to the fabric of life. A critical mass was reached in the literary world, and barriers fell, though usually with a good deal of official resistance. In our present age, it is perhaps difficult to appreciate that Joyce's *Ulysses* was censored as pornographic (Hemingway himself was instrumental in sneaking the first copies into the United States); that the serialized version of Hemingway's *A Farewell to Arms* was banned in Boston; or that one story intended for *In Our Time* had to be removed at the publisher's request because it briefly depicted a sex scene. The seamy, the violent, the painful, the shameful, the grotesque, the ironic — all are represented heavily in this early book. Indeed, in his first decade as an author Hemingway did epic work in dismantling the genteel tradition by publishing stories treating such subjects as date rape, venereal disease, male homosexuality, lesbianism, bisexuality, sexual fetishes, incest (perceived, if not real), out-of-wedlock pregnancy, self-castration, small-town prostitution, drunkenness, drug addiction, racial conflict, insanity, gangsterism, fixed horse races, intended murder, executions, and, many times over, the violence of modern mechanized warfare. Among the literati who frequented Montparnasse, Hemingway found admirers for his frank treatment of "our time"; but it is not surprising that his pious and sentimental mother would admonish him that *The Sun Also Rises* was "the filthiest book of the year," nor that his prudish father would insist on returning six precious copies of an earlier book that he had ordered from Paris.

The book Clarence Hemingway returned was *in our time,* printed in an edition of 170 copies in March 1924 by Bill Bird's Three Mountains Press in Paris. Its eighteen vignettes consist of the sixteen that remain as the numbered and italicized "chapters" in *In Our Time,* published commercially by Boni and Liveright of New York on 5 October 1925, and two, titled "A Very Short Story" and "The Revolutionist," that are given the status and ordinary typeface of full-fledged stories in the 1925 edition. As originally conceived, *In Our Time* was to include the story "Up in Michigan," the story that Boni and Liveright would not publish because it depicts a sex scene.[10] This loss was actually a gain, as Hemingway replaced "Up in Michigan" with "The Battler," a new — and superior — story about Nick Adams. In 1930 another story, titled "Introduction by the Author," was added when the volume was brought out by Heming-

---

[10] This story, originally intended to be placed second, after "Indian Camp," is now readily available in *The Short Stories* and in *The Nick Adams Stories* (1972), compiled posthumously for Scribner's by Philip Young. On first reading "Up in Michigan," Stein had warned Hemingway that it was *"inaccrochable.* That means it is like a picture that a painter paints and then he cannot hang it" (Baker, *A Life Story* 87). Curiously, it is also one of only two stories to survive Hadley Hemingway's famous loss of Ernest's other manuscripts during a train trip in 1922.

way's new publisher, Scribner's; that story was first headed with its present title, "On the Quai at Smyrna," in the 1938 story collection on called the *First Forty-Nine Stories*. It was also given that title in the 1955 reissue of *In Our Time*. Since then, the volume has appeared as it is presently constituted.[11]

---

[11] Michael Reynolds has provided a detailed account of the publication history of *In Our Time* in his essay "Hemingway's *In Our Time:* The Biography of a Book" (1995). I follow him in stressing the ex-post-facto nature of its organization. See also Susan Garland Mann's chapter "Ernest Hemingway's *In Our Time*" in her *The Short Story Cycle* (1989).

3: Continuities and Discontinuities of Form: *In Our Time* as Modernist Achievement

WHILE MANY IMPORTANT CONTINUITIES can be found in *In Our Time*, anyone who has read it will testify that the experience is anything but smoothly continuous. Rather, the book has a fragmented feel; and, with the *in our time* vignettes italicized and inserted as "chapters," it even has a fragmented *look*. While Hemingway's precise intentions for the book can never be completely reconstructed, several important statements by him on the subject exist. Simultaneously thought-provoking and confusing, these statements must be taken into account, though they need not be granted the final word on the volume's form. One need not be certain of the author's intentions in order to describe what it is like to read the book or to make judgments about the way the stories interact. As it turns out, an adequate description of the volume's form requires a dual eye, one ready to accommodate the traditional narrative features of the book but also to apply a more truly modern aesthetic.

When he began to think about compiling his first book of short stories, Hemingway had before him the notable models of James Joyce and Sherwood Anderson, each of whom had written a new sort of collection, a closely knit sequence of stories that was not truly a novel but had novel-like qualities.[1] Many short-story volumes, of course, achieve a degree of unity, and in some of the best collections the reader's experience of the volume as a whole is greater than the sum of its parts. But the story sequence differs from more-traditional story collections in that its individual stories generate far greater meaning and complexity through their interactions. Such modern collections as Joyce's *Dubliners* (1914), Anderson's *Winesburg, Ohio*, Faulkner's *Go Down, Moses* (1942), and Katherine Ann Porter's *The*

---

[1] What I refer to as a story sequence has also been called a short-story cycle, a short-story composite, or an integrated short-story collection.

Leaning Tower (1944), for example, demonstrate a high degree of intentionally achieved interrelatedness that distinguishes them from the ordinary miscellaneous collection of stories.

Many critics seem to take for granted that *In Our Time* is a story sequence, and it does achieve the necessary degree of interrelatedness to merit this classification. It is *the way* that Hemingway's volume achieves the status of story sequence that is of primary interest, however, for the case is not simple and straightforward. A high degree of intended formal unity does exist, but it arrived relatively late in the process of the volume's composition. Literary history has its happy accidents, and while by no means completely accidental in conception, the aesthetic form the volume achieves has a great deal of the ex post facto about it. What Hemingway himself termed the volume's aesthetic "unity" should in large part be measured by the sort of complex, juxtapositional aesthetics that are applicable to cubist paintings, for, while *In Our Time* exhibits certain tendencies of a traditional sequential narrative, much of the book's effect cannot be explained using only these terms.

Hemingway achieves some of the geographic and temporal unity that Joyce and Anderson imposed on *Dubliners* and *Winesburg, Ohio,* each of which confines itself to one locale, and each of which demonstrates a stronger tendency toward depicting a broader cross-section of the population than Hemingway's volume. Still, *In Our Time* begins in this regional, time-and-place vein, with young Nick in the Michigan woods for five stories. But then Hemingway veers off to other places and other characters before returning to Nick, who ends the volume where he began: in the Michigan woods. The circularity attained with "Big Two-Hearted River" was important to Hemingway and clearly was an intentional aspect of the book's creation, giving the volume something of the regional consistency usually associated with story sequences. But the widely flung stories in the second half of the book break off from the initially sustained unity of place.

Likewise, the volume demonstrates some of the unity associated with story sequences in regard to character. Story sequences frequently feature a high incidence of character recurrence from story to story or contain a central character who serves as a sort of narrative backbone in the volume, as Anderson's George Willard does in *Winesburg, Ohio*. Apart from Nick, however, there are few recurring characters in Hemingway's volume. Dr. Adams appears in two stories and is mentioned in a third; Bill appears in two stories as a foil for Nick; and Maera the bullfighter appears in two consecutive vignettes. Some of the unnamed narrators of the vignettes — the ironic and understated British officer(s), for example — may well be the same character, though there is no way of knowing for sure. This is not much by way of character recurrence.

On the other hand, Nick does appear in seven of the fifteen stories and in one vignette, suggesting that the book be viewed in light of the bildungsroman tradition, wherein the development of a young person is episodically and chronologically recounted. The participation of *In Our Time* in this tradition is reinforced by the order in which the non-Nick stories are placed (though the dicey question of "My Old Man" must be acknowledged), for they correspond with Nick's development. Some of them, such as "A Very Short Story" and "Soldier's Home," have characters who, while they are not Nick, share important characteristics with him, so that the volume can almost be said to show the development of an ur-character, a (male) representative figure of "our time." Indeed, despite Nick's on-again, off-again presence, his only partly fulfilled role as the book's protagonist, he is a much fuller and more interesting character in his own right than George Willard, who is nominally onstage more frequently in Anderson's collection. Much of Nick's equivocal status as central character can be explained in terms of the composition of the stories: Hemingway did not immediately conceive of Nick as a central figure but came progressively to see his centrality.[2]

Thus, the volume's status as a story sequence must be hedged with qualifiers such as *partly, some but not all,* and *on the one hand, ... on the other hand,* .... This status must be hedged even further if Hemingway's intentions and methods of composition are taken into account. And, finally, there is the all-important question of the vignettes. "Tools of self-instruction," Charles A. Fenton called them in his early study of Hemingway's apprentice years (228), and this

[2] See Benson 108.

they were — and sharply honed tools, at that — but they have a status in the volume that is much more important than this phrase would indicate. How does their fragmentary nature affect our consideration of the volume as a short-story sequence? Is their aesthetic effect primarily to unify or to disrupt? To begin with the question of Hemingway's intentions: he had written all of the vignettes and many of the stories before he began to make inquiries about publishing a volume. We can be sure that he had entertained hopes of a collection while he wrote them, but that does not mean that he wrote the stories with a specific organization in mind. It seems more likely that he wrote the stories he was interested in writing, the stories that he was ready to write at a given time, no doubt cognizant of various overlapping themes and of Nick's potential to hold the stories together. Afterward he would seek to impose the best order that he could on the material he had ready to hand.[3]

After the fact, in two now-famous letters Hemingway not only claimed that the volume has unity but implied that the unity is the product of conscious, careful construction. He specifically maintained that the vignettes had originally been written with the idea that they would eventually become "chapters" in a larger book. This belated assertion would seem to be false, since at no time during their composition does he refer to this ultimate intention. Indeed, much of the *In Our Time* material had already appeared in little magazines before the volume's publication, and the vignettes had been written with specific small-press targets in mind. These considerations argue against Hemingway's having had a definitive master plan for the volume from the outset.

Still, the letters are quite enlightening. The first was written on 12 September 1924 to Edward J. O'Brien, who edited the annual *Best Short Stories* volumes, the second on 18 October 1924 to the

---

[3] Hemingway's letters are the primary resource for piecing together his composition of the stories and inferring his intentions for the volume as a whole. Besides the letters and scholarly biographies, the reader is referred to Mann, to Smith, and to Reynolds's "Biography of a Book" for considerations of dating, composition, and organization.

eminent literary critic Edmund Wilson. To O'Brien, Hemingway described his book in terms partly cinematic and partly musical:

> I have written 14 stories and have a book ready to publish. It is to be called In Our Time and one of the chapters of the In Our Time [i.e., the vignettes published as *in our time*] I sent you comes in between each story. That was what I originally wrote them for, chapter headings. All the stories have a certain unity, the first 5 are in Michigan, starting with the Up In Michigan, which you know and in between each one comes bang! the In Our Time [i.e., *in our time*]. . . . I've tried to do it so you get the close up very quietly but absolutely solid and the real thing but very close, and then through it all between every story comes the rhythm of the in our time chapters (*SL* 123).

While this often-cited letter does not provide a detailed explanation of how "all the stories have a certain unity," it does seem correct, though vague, in all but its assertion of Hemingway's original intentions regarding the vignettes. One is left to wonder whether Hemingway uses these inexplicit critical terms merely because he does not want to seem to play the role of self-explaining author in an informal letter, or whether their imprecision reveals a still-shaky conception of the volume's form. Whichever the case may be, Hemingway describes the stories as "quiet" when they are not at all quiet emotionally; and the surface action of stories such as "Indian Camp," "The Doctor and the Doctor's Wife," and "The Battler" can hardly be said to be quiet, either. But insofar as *quiet* is meant to refer to Hemingway's understated narration in the face of extreme events and the development of his art of implication, the word would seem to be accurate. The stories indulge in no plot fireworks, and they tend to end in a minor key rather than with an ostentatious surprise. Likewise, the vignettes do produce a "bang!" with their highly honed, economical descriptions of essentially sensational incidents. Finally, Hemingway recognizes that the vignettes themselves have a certain internal logic and feel ("the rhythm"). Indeed, they exercise an influence on the tone of the book that is out of all proportion to their collective length.

    In the second letter, to Wilson, Hemingway again uses an ocular metaphor:

Finished the book of 14 stories with a chapter on [i.e., of] *In Our Time* [i.e., the vignettes published as *in our time*] between each story — that is the way they were meant to go — to give the picture of the whole between examining it in detail. Like looking with your eyes at something, say a passing coast line, and then looking at it with 15X binoculars. Or rather, maybe, looking at it and then going in and living in it — and then coming out and looking at it again. (*SL* 128)

Setting aside the misleading repetition of his original intentions for the vignettes, one is confronted with the confused grammar of "to give the picture of the whole between examining it it detail." Hemingway seems to be saying that the vignettes provide a general depiction of the times ("the picture of the whole," "a passing coast line"), while the stories provide detailed, exemplary illustrations of those times ("examining it in detail," "looking at it with 15X binoculars"). The last sentence also hints at the detachment, the coldly observational style ("looking at it") that typifies the vignettes. While it might seem ironic that the shortest pieces in the book are meant to carry the burden of delineating an era, Hemingway is correct in saying that they do so. He is also correct in assuming that the reader will feel a greater emotional attachment ("going in and living in it") to the stories than to the vignettes ("looking at it"). While they have been refined so as to achieve the status of enduring art, the vignettes have their roots in journalism, in topics and events Hemingway believed were representative of the postwar world his grown-up characters and his readers alike had to confront. Much of the weight of the volume's title rests on the vignettes, for it is they, more than anything, that define the particularly modern aspects on view in the book. "Give us peace in our time," reads the *Book of Common Prayer*, but the action in this, and in Hemingway's subsequent books, makes clear that such prayers are not about to receive a swift answer.

There is one more letter that sheds light on Hemingway's conception of the volume. Worried by reports that his publisher wanted to remove the vignettes and "Indian Camp," he wrote to John Dos Passos that he felt "all shot to hell about it. Of course they cant do it because the stuff is so tight and hard and every thing hangs on every thing else and it would all just be shot up shit creek" [*sic*] (22/4/1925: *SL* 157). So although he had not given consistent thought to the final form of the volume while he composed each story, by the time he wrote this letter Hemingway had come to feel artistically attached to the volume's organization. (He was also un-doubtedly anxious that the volume not be made any slimmer.) We also know, from the same letter to Dos Passos, that when he was forced to replace "Up in Michigan" Hemingway did not simply stick its substitute, "The Battler," in the first slot, where the censored story had been, but moved it back to the fifth position, where it more sensibly fits into the chronological pattern of Nick's develop-ment.

Hemingway's insistence on unity has led many readers to try to view the volume solely through traditional narrative paradigms. But the word *unity*, with its rather classical sound and its connotations of proportion and symmetry and well-balanced correspondences, seems misapplied when it is weighed against the actual experience of read-ing the volume. It would be as well to invoke a different modernist critical watchword — *complexity* — to describe the collection, for the volume paradoxically carries the feel of fragmentation and indetermi-nacy while retaining a high degree of interrelatedness. Above all, it is the inclusion of the vignettes that complicates the book. It is they that demand that another critical yardstick, in addition to narrative unity, be used to measure the book. It is the vignettes that give the book a complexity not achieved by Hemingway's predecessors such as Joyce (in his *Dubliners* phase) and Anderson. And it is the vi-gnettes that turn the volume from a partly realized example of a uni-fied story sequence into a casebook of modernist juxtapository techniques. One senses the influence of Pound here, for he favored poetic sequences that lacked clear connective material and traditional guideposts to the reader. The inclusion of the vignettes, in typical modernist fashion, demands new reading strategies. Their unpre-dictable movements through time and space, their shifts in narrative voice, their *in medias res* quality, even the fragmented look they give to the pages of *In Our Time* call forth the terms of modern art. They impose an alogical quality on the whole; yet, the texts formulate, much like a cubist painting, their own sort of meaningfulness.

While important parallels exist between the aesthetics of cubism and the execution of *In Our Time,* one would be hard pressed to prove their existence on the basis of authorial intentions.[4] Whereas both Hemingway and his fictional alter ego, Nick Adams, make explicit references to adopting Cézanne's techniques, neither mentions cubist artists. Still, by the 1920s cubist aesthetic principles were an established part of the Parisian ambiance, and Hemingway often breathed deeply inside the experimentalist oxygen tent that was Gertrude Stein's apartment. He was not altogether ignorant of modern art before he arrived in Paris (he had seen the famous Armory Show when it traveled to Chicago), but in Paris his interest in painting of all sorts, including the avant-garde, increased greatly and with profound consequences.

From Cézanne, Hemingway learned, in part, that nature need not be painted as a mere record of what the eye sees but that a well-selected detail could stand for the whole. He decided never to indulge in the "backdrop" sort of description provided by writers of previous generations. Piling up details was not the same as telling the truth, and it would have led not only to a deadness in his prose but to falseness. Verbal photographs were not needed, certainly gilding was not, but selection was — and, even more than selection, construction. "Prose is architecture, not interior decoration," he wrote in *Death in the Afternoon,* "and the baroque is over" (170). This statement can be used to buttress discussions of Hemingway's desire for verbal simplification ("the baroque is over") and as an animadversion on the genteel writer, to whose overthrow Hemingway had become committed (prose is "not interior decoration"). But it should also be taken as an indication of his interest in constructed forms ("prose *is* architecture").

---

[4] While he does not specifically delineate cubist aesthetics in Hemingway's books, Alfred Kazin engagingly treats the importance of painting to Hemingway (see especially 366–373). Jacqueline Vaught Brogan and Elizabeth Dewberry Vaughn have written about Hemingway's relationship to cubism per se, while Michael Reynolds has downplayed its importance (see especially *Young Hemingway* 158–162).

One key to cubism, as to *In Our Time,* is simultaneity, the representation of multiple perspectives on the same canvas. A cubist painting is fragmented, but the fragments are not meaningless; they acquire multiple meanings from the context of the entire painting. A fragmented violin is deliberately irrealist, and it presents a puzzling picture to one trained to expect naturalistic representation, but it is still a violin. The vignettes of *In Our Time* can be viewed in the same vein. Taken individually they are literarily worthy, but it is in their aggregate interplay that one finds their true richness of meaning. One important way of viewing the vignettes is to see them as studies in violence, each of which refracts the other vignettes, and each of which is also apt to play off one or more of the longer stories. Thus, for example, the retreat depicted in "Chapter II" emphasizes dehumanization and the horrible, while the British narrator of "Chapter III" first feels an amused thrill, then guilt over his easy "potting" of the enemy; in the face of danger Villalta's triumph is noble, controlled, even sexual, while the criminal Sam Cardinella disgustingly epitomizes cowardice in the face of death; and so on. Each vignette presents a brief take on the violence of "our time," fragmentary in its own right but contributing to the larger "picture of the whole." Thus, the volume cannot be fully appreciated using only the aesthetic criteria applied to realistic fiction any more than a cubist painting can be understood using only the criteria derived from Renaissance Masters. Although Hemingway never precisely spelled out what he meant by *unity* when he declared that his volume of stories has it, what he created embodies the new modernistic unity, like that found in a cubist painting.

4: A Reading of the Stories

"On the Quai at Smyrna": An Introduction to Method

WHEN FIRST PUBLISHED, *In Our Time* did not begin with "On the Quai at Smyrna." In 1930 the famous Scribner's editor Maxwell Perkins asked Hemingway to write an introduction to the volume for its first reissue and to send along "new material" for inclusion. Deep into the composition of *Death in the Afternoon* and apparently desirous of keeping the earlier volume's contents all "of the same period," Hemingway declined Perkins's request. Instead, he suggested that Edmund Wilson, America's preeminent literary critic, be asked to provide an introduction, which Wilson did. Hemingway also suggested that "The Smyrna chapter can go as an Introduction by The Author," which it did (Bruccoli 147). This short piece, then, should be viewed as a work deliberately chosen by Hemingway to (re)introduce his initial foray into the world of modern writing.

The story was finished shortly after the initial publication of *In Our Time* and was likely begun while Hemingway was writing the other vignettes that would become the "chapters" of that work.[1] "On the Quai at Smyrna" provides a fitting and typically indirect introduction to the stories of Nick Adams's boyhood that follow, for it depicts in miniature the violence and senselessness of the modern world in which Nick will have to make his way. Its conflation of

---

[1] For the dating of this story's composition, and for much information on the composition history of all of the stories in the volume, I am indebted to Paul Smith's thorough and indispensable work. Hemingway's further thoughts on the question of an introduction, as well as his concerns about the possible libelousness of certain stories in *In Our Time,* can be read in his letters to Perkins (*Selected Letters* 326–328, Bruccoli 144–149, 150–152, 155).

birth and death anticipates the similar conflation that Nick will witness in "Indian Camp," preparing the reader for the volume's modernist juxtapository aesthetic — that is, for the manner in which
stories and vignettes play off of one another. The Greco-Turkish
War setting will itself be repeated in three vignettes, and the story's
depiction of the horrors of modern war is not only a central concern
of several early vignettes but also occupies a dominant thematic position in the second half of the volume. Finally, the story provides a
gemlike example of Hemingway's ability to define sharply, in a few
words, an anonymous yet distinctive narrative voice. He achieves a
characterization at once pointed and remarkably full without resort-
ing to authorial intrusion and without the use of a single adjective to
describe the main character. Instead, he allows small details to accu-
mulate, gradually and indirectly revealing the sort of man the British
officer is.

After the passage of seven decades the historical particulars of
"On the Quai at Smyrna" have become obscure. Hemingway covered the Greco-Turkish war as a correspondent, and though he was
not present at the Greek and Armenian retreat through Smyrna
(now Turkish Izmir), he was familiar with its inhuman aspects. By
the end of the First World War the displacement of mass popula-
tions, the brutality toward soldiers and civilians alike, and the *in-
extremis* situations forced on people by war — here the need to give
birth in the dark hold of a ship — had already come to typify modern geopolitical conduct. Man's inhumanity to man had reached
enormous proportions in the new century. The story has the look of
a nightmarish surrealist painting, but the nightmare in this instance
was a reality.

From a technical point of view the story's primary effect is to
prefigure the volume's experimental, modernistic qualities: it is a
challenging piece, cryptic because it withholds information that
normally would be provided in a traditional realist narrative. Like
other important modernist works, the volume calls for a model of
reading that is at variance both with popular genre formulas and
with the narrative demands typical of serious nineteenth-century
works of fiction. The storytelling strategy is not straightforward.
"On the Quai at Smyrna" begins abruptly, with the reader seemingly

eavesdropping on a snippet from a war-story session and lacking a larger context in which to frame the events. At the grammatical level the reader is confronted with a welter of antecedentless pronouns to sort out by a process of inference. The story is shot through with ironic threads and is delivered by a storyteller who is referred to only as "he" but who seems to have been a British officer at Smyrna. The narrator who frames the story ("The strange thing was, he said . . .") remains unknown, as does the "he" whose voice then comes to dominate the narration (11). "He" implies that the narrator has shared some facets of his experience ("You remember the harbor"), and the reader, searching for answers to some basic narrative questions, has the feeling of listening in on a conversation between two old war buddies (12).

The story that "he" relates is an absurdist tale of a vindictive Turkish officer who, in the midst of victory and with suffering and destruction all around, insists that a British sailor be punished for insulting him. Happy to see his false sense of honor repaired at anyone's expense, the Turk feels "topping" about the severe punishment that he believes will be meted out to the wholly innocent, "inoffensive chap" he has targeted as the offender cum scapegoat (11). The British storyteller obviously finds the incident insanely petty, given the larger context of tragic events being played out on the quai. He repeats this ironic incident, all the while adopting his own ironic rhetorical devices in an apparent effort simultaneously to recount the brutality he has witnessed and also to keep it at a psychically safe distance. The chaotic retreat is the only thing in his life that has plagued him with nightmares, he says, defending himself from the unprocessable with a stiff upper lip and ironically phrased sarcasm: "It was all a pleasant business. My word yes a most pleasant business" (12).

Later in the volume "A Very Short Story" and "Mr. and Mrs. Elliot" again feature heavily ironic narrators, but with less success. In those stories the irony is spoken from a superior, attacking position, while here it is used for self-protection. As his dreams reveal, the officer has been through more than he can handle, has witnessed too many barbaric acts, and must feign a callousness he perhaps wishes he actually had. He will not allow himself to express his horror straightforwardly; yet, after all that he has seen, he retains his sensitivity, as is shown by his admission that the Greeks' cruelty to their pack mules still haunts his memory. The development of a strongly characterized storyteller goes a long way toward making "On the Quai at Smyrna" one of Hemingway's successful ventures into world-weary irony. So does the fact that the story is told at one remove, framed, however briefly, at the outset by the nominal narrator who tells us, "The strange thing was, he said. . ." (11). During his Parisian internship Hemingway had read and admired Joseph Conrad, master of the framed story. In its ironic stance, its technical virtuosity, and its depiction of the 1920s world, this brief story serves as a fitting introduction to the thirty-two pieces of fiction that follow.

Before the War: The Young Nick Adams

"Indian Camp" is the first of five consecutive Nick Adams stories. He is a young boy when he accompanies his physician father and his uncle George to an Indian camp in a remote area. His father has been summoned to aid in a protracted labor that had begun two days before their arrival. With Nick close by and able to look on, Dr. Adams performs a Caesarian section, saving both mother and child, even though the only instruments at his disposal are a jackknife and some fishing leader. During the surgery Dr. Adams tries to explain to Nick what he is doing and why he must maintain his composure in the face of the Indian woman's screams of pain. The men then discover that during the operation the husband, lying nearby in his bunk, has quietly committed suicide by slitting his throat, putting a quick end to the doctor's feeling of triumph over crude conditions. As they row back across the lake, Nick asks his father simply phrased but deep questions about birth and death.

"Indian Camp" is one of the volume's best stories, in great part because the mysteries at its heart can never be solved. Though Nick is a young boy, no one, including the reader, can assume a superior position to him. We, too, are left wondering why the husband killed himself; his motive seems to be a submerged part of the story's iceberg, known to the writer and purposely "left out." While the grotesque suicide comes as a shock, Hemingway has provided brief and subtle foreshadowing for it. On the arrival of Nick, Dr. Adams, and Uncle George in the cabin, we learn that the man has wounded his foot with an axe and that a bad smell (of death?) is associated with him. More richly, the ill-fated husband registers some of the story's deeper ironies. The conjunction of birth and death central to the piece was introduced in "On the Quai at Smyrna" and will also be present in the vignette ("Chapter II") that follows. Indeed, the interrelationship of sex and various sorts of death, both literal and metaphorical, forms a thematic nexus that is present in more than half of the stories in *In Our Time*. In "Indian Camp" wife and husband incorporate these respective themes, right down to the postures of their bodies. As the men and Nick enter the cabin, the wife is lying "in the lower bunk, very big under a quilt. Her head was turned to one side" (16). Her husband's presence in his own bunk and his wounded foot are mentioned immediately after the description of the woman. After the birth the husband is discovered dead, under a blanket, lying on his side "with his face toward the wall," a position that is in counterpoint to that of his wife when "discovered" in labor. Thus Hemingway ironically choreographs birth and death. But the story contains another grisly irony of parallel action: just as the woman's screams reach their apogee, just as the doctor is declaring his scientific detachment from her screams, just as he is unwrapping the crude instruments with which he will perform the operation, bringing her relief and giving life — just at this moment the husband takes out his own instrument, the razor, and slits his throat from ear to ear. Ironically, this tool would have made for an easier and cleaner operation than the jackknife the doctor is forced to use; but instead, it is horribly employed in taking life rather than in delivering it.

Understandably, birth and death remain vague and puzzling to Nick. Yet, he is obviously impressed by seeing each in such a terribly vivid form. His final dialogue with his father reveals that there has been too much in the night's experiences for him to comprehend:

> "Do ladies always have such a hard time having babies?" Nick asked.
> "No, that was very, very exceptional."
> "Why did he kill himself, Daddy?"

"I don't know, Nick. He couldn't stand things, I guess."
. . . "Is dying hard, Daddy?"
"No, I think it's pretty easy, Nick. It all depends."
. . . In the early morning on the lake sitting in the stern of the
boat with his father rowing, he felt quite sure that he would never
die. (19)

Some readers find Dr. Adams an inadequate guide for Nick: they
point to his lack of foresight in bringing Nick along in the first place
or in asking the boy to "assist," or they judge his answers to his
son's troubled questions insufficient. Indeed, Dr. Adams himself expresses regret for having brought Nick along, even though circumstances seem to have left him little choice: he could not have left
young Nick behind, alone, in this remote area. As it stands, the story
implies clearly enough the remoteness of the setting — for example,
when the doctor mentions that the regional nurse will probably be
able to arrive with the proper supplies by the following noon (18) —
but the initial draft of the story included an opening scene that made
it explicit that the doctor, Uncle George, and Nick are camping in
an isolated area. Hemingway eventually dropped this scene in favor
of the typically modernist *in medias res* first sentence, an early instance of his "leaving something out" to strengthen a story.[2] But
knowledge of this deleted beginning reinforces the fact that the incident is sudden and unforeseen and that the setting is far removed
from proper medical facilities, all of which compels Nick's father to
make do. Thus, judged in his role as a father, at most Dr. Adams can
be accused of being too single-mindedly and scientistically devoted
to the medical problem at hand and, perhaps, of displaying a too
ready postpartum self-congratulation — both minor foibles under
the circumstances. Dr. Adams seems to want to instruct his son in

[2] The excised opening also depicts Nick as feeling powerfully and for the
first time the reality that he will some day die. Hemingway may have
judged this vivid epiphany to have been too heavily at odds with Nick's
denial of his mortality at the end of "Indian Camp." The deleted portion
of the story, which is written with skill and feeling, is included as "Three
Shots" in *The Nick Adams Stories* (1972).

the ways of methodical, scientific medicine: "Her screams are not important," he tells Nick. "I don't hear them because they are not important" (16). As he pulls the baby from the mother's womb, he asks how Nick likes being "an interne." But the overriding fact remains that the doctor succeeds in saving two lives under extremely difficult circumstances, and he must deal with his son's confusion and fear as best he can given the limited alternatives. He tries to keep Nick occupied with the necessary duties at hand.

The doctor can likewise be forgiven his elation and his slightly pompous cliché about "the proud father" being "the worst sufferer in these little affairs" (18). What is more ambiguous — indeed, troubling — about the doctor is not his treatment of his son but the seemingly small regard he displays for his patient: his bedside manner is notable by its absence. Perhaps the extremity of the emergency and the necessity to perform under such crude conditions account for the lack of comforting and sympathetic words from doctor to patient. If the price for focusing on the job to be done is an outwardly callous demeanor, then it is undoubtedly a price worth paying, for, again, the doctor saves two lives. Whether Dr. Adams's all-business manner would have been softer had his suffering patient been white is a question the story raises but does not provide a sufficient basis to answer. Potentially more important than the doctor's demeanor is his rather swift departure, leaving behind a postoperative and newly widowed patient. After such a protracted labor, and considering the crude surgical improvisations he has had to make, should the doctor not have maintained a longer bedside vigil? Again, whether this seeming too-slight a regard for his patient's welfare is racially motivated, or whether it arises from the doctor's conflicting duties as a father to his young son, cannot be answered on the basis of this story, nor even on the basis of what we will subsequently see of Dr. Adams.[3]

---

[3] Uncle George's attitude to Indians lies just beneath the surface, emerging in the "damn squaw bitch" that he blurts out on being bitten by the Indian woman in the throes of her labor pains. In future Nick Adams stories it will be made clear that Dr. Adams has at least a collector's interest in

Thus, this story, like the next one, airs the weaknesses and failures of Dr. Adams. The real horror of the story, however, arises from its ironic foundation, not from any callousness on the doctor's part. It arises from circumstances that he could not control and from an action that he could not have foreseen. The doctor has no choice but to bring Nick along and then try to make the best of the fact, just as he is forced to improvise a Caesarian section with implements taken from a tackle box rather than from a physician's black bag. Since Nick's innocence is confronted with brutal experience, it may seem natural to view "Indian Camp" as an initiation story; but it is not only Nick who is initiated. Dr. Adams seems to learn from the experience that he must keep things at his son's level. Expecting him to be Daddy's "interne" during the operation was asking too much. Realizing his mistake, the doctor carefully frames suitable replies to Nick's questions at the story's end. Nick is quite young, and keeping the answers short and simple shows Dr. Adams to be a good father, not a self-centered or inattentive one. If the doctor does not have answers to the metaphysical dimensions of Nick's questions about birth and death, he can be forgiven for joining the rest of the human race, who likewise do not. If he does have deeper thoughts on these matters, he is wise not to confuse his child with age-inappropriate philosophizing that would speak neither to Nick's intellectual development nor to the boy's emotional needs.

What is most remarkable about the ending is not, therefore, any possible failure on the doctor's part but, rather, Nick's response to what he has witnessed. He is first confused, then youthfully complacent. His confusion reveals itself in his question about the Indian man's suicide ("Why did he kill himself, Daddy?"), which follows immediately, and as a non sequitur, his father's answer to his question about the difficult nature of giving birth. The rest of *In Our Time* can be said to take root in the yawning gap between Nick's two questions about birth and death. Birth and death each reveals itself to be grimly and painfully difficult to the inexperienced Nick. The rest of the volume will prove to him that life itself — everything

---

Indian culture. However one may characterize Dr. Adams's attitude to Indians, it certainly seems to be less crudely bigoted than George's.

that comprises that for-now-unquestioned gap between birth and death — will be a series of difficult initiations.

Hemingway chooses to stick close to the child's point of view throughout the story, including the ending. No all-knowing narrator steps forward to reveal what the events have meant to Nick or to relate an older Nick's reflections on this grim night. For now, Nick slips into complacency as he returns with his father across the lake. Trailing his hand in the water, comforted by nature, lulled into reassurance by the rhythms of his father's competent rowing, he returns to the child's confidence in his own immortality. As he grows older, it will become progressively harder to smooth over traumatic events. Here immaturity aids Nick, and here, as in the next story, father and son receive nature's psychic balm after turbulent events.

"The Doctor and the Doctor's Wife" also deals with Indians and axes and is also a story wherein we observe Nick's father under duress. Like "Indian Camp," it shows the doctor to be only partly responsible for the calamitous ending to an event that escapes his control. He is much put upon, first by hired help, then by his wife. In this story, which in many ways is a mirror image of "Indian Camp," the Indians leave their camp to come to the doctor's cabin; just as he brought his sharp implements to the Indian camp, they bring theirs to his house. Dick Boulton walks to the Adamses' lakefront home ominously carrying three axes under his arm. He has been hired by the doctor to cut driftwood and is accompanied by his son Eddy and Billy Tabeshaw. Dick owes the doctor money for curing his wife of pneumonia but apparently resents having to work off the debt. He quickly picks a quarrel with Dr. Adams, pointedly repeating that the driftwood is actually the property of a logging company. The doctor allows the bigger and tougher Dick to provoke him into issuing a threat he will never have the nerve to act upon, so Dick is successful not only in dodging the doctor's job of work but also in humiliating him. Thus, for the second story in a row the doctor's successful treatment of an Indian's wife has an unsatisfactory ending. Adams retreats to his home, there to be met by his wife's disbelief in his opinion that Dick picked the fight to get out of working off the debt. With imagery that is consistent with the doctor's present exasperation and simultaneously deftly metaphorical of a deeper nexus of repressed violence and sexuality, Hemingway depicts Dr. Adams sitting on his bed, loading, unloading, and cleaning his shotgun, pumping out the "heavy yellow shells" so that they are "scattered on the bed" (26). Still angry, the doctor leaves for a walk in the woods, accompanied by Nick.

Whereas the events of "Indian Camp" are inherently sensational, this story is built on a mundane incident that quickly becomes highly charged. The piece is rendered vividly, but beyond the surface vividness one sees the capacity for emotional resonance that is built into Hemingway's art of implication. The story is structured by two conflicts, one plainly apparent and one subterranean. The doctor's conflict with Dick Boulton must be viewed in light of the long-standing cultural clash between white and Native American men, a conflict in which the latter have usually come out the losers. But as enacted here the conflict is quick and loud, and its immediate source is readily identifiable. The second conflict, between the doctor and his wife, is quiet, subtle, undoubtedly of long standing, and irremediable.

Although the scene between Dick and the doctor takes up more than half of the story, and although their conflict is the more overtly dramatic one, the story's title implies that the quieter conflict between Dr. and Mrs. Adams is actually more ruinous. So the doctor, humiliated as he is by Dick Boulton, is actually more damaged by the humiliations and emasculations meted out by his wife. As he sits on his bed (in a room separate from hers, we are told), pumping shells into and out of his shotgun, one wonders whom he would most like to turn it on — Dick, his wife, or, possibly, himself. Hiding out in her darkened room, guided by her Christian Scientist literature, and smugly certain of her own naive and limited worldview, she apparently rules the roost:

> The doctor went out on the porch. The screen door slammed behind him. He heard his wife catch her breath when the door slammed.
> "Sorry," he said, outside her window with the blinds drawn. (102–103)

A physician married to a woman who does not believe in medical science, Dr. Adams has apparently done a great deal of apologizing for himself over the years. Doing so seems to come as second nature now, even in the midst of his other humiliations. The willful naivete of a sentimentally religious woman hiding out in her darkened room cannot be overcome. The doctor and his wife will undoubtedly continue to sleep in separate beds. In "Now I Lay Me," a story written after the publication of *In Our Time*, Dr. Adams again suppresses his anger in the face of his wife's high-handed obliviousness. She has deliberately destroyed his collection of Indian arrowheads, and once again the doctor's shotgun is conspicuously present in his moment of angry discovery.

Dr. Adams wrests one small and surreptitious victory at the end of "The Doctor and the Doctor's Wife." Charged by his wife to send Nick back to her if he happens to encounter their son, the doctor purposely finds the boy, then overrides her instructions by allowing Nick to accompany him on his walk in the woods. Just as "Indian Camp" ended with father and son retreating into the solace of nature, rowing alone together in their boat on the lake, so "The Doctor and the Doctor's Wife" ends with a father-son flight to nature, this time a deliberate excursion into the woods, where the doctor apparently intends to salve his wounds in an environment more conducive to the exertion of self-control: "It was cool in the woods even on such a hot day" (27).

It is unclear how well Nick appreciates the moral ambiguity of his father's appropriation of the logs; moreover, the degree to which he is aware of his father's double humiliation remains uncertain. But he does appear to be well attuned to his father's emotional state, as we see when he expresses his desire to accompany the doctor on the walk rather than go to see what his mother wants. Some readers have assumed that Nick witnesses his father's humiliations; the story does provide slight, though certainly not conclusive, evidence that he is present at the beach for the confrontation between his father and Dick, but none that he is within earshot of his parents' conversation.[4] What seems most likely is that Nick witnesses the episode with

[4] See Joseph M. Flora, *Ernest Hemingway: A Study of the Short Fiction*, 18.

Dick and retreats into the woods, and thus that he does not overhear his father's exchange with his mother. Seeing his father approaching in the woods, he intuits the doctor's troubled state of mind and falls into sync with his father's efforts to escape Mrs. Adams, a woman who seems bent on infantilizing both husband and son. Touchingly, Nick offers to show his defeated father where some black squirrels dwell. For now, Dr. Adams has left his gun behind; the presence of nature and of his son will apparently be sufficient emotional salve.

Meanwhile, Dick receives no comeuppance for his rude aggressiveness. Unlike the doctor, whose brief moment of triumph in "Indian Camp" is shattered by the chastening tragedy of the husband's suicide, Dick seems here to have won a clear, if small, victory. Making a joke in Ojibwa, he walks away, studiously failing to shut the doctor's gate as he leaves the premises. Perhaps more meaningful to consider, however, is the context of white-Indian relationships that occupies an important place in these two stories, which are, in many ways, counterpoints of one another.[5] In "Indian Camp" Dr. Adams's superiority is based on his status as man of medical science. The Indians have sought him out to accomplish what they cannot, and the successes he achieves are based on his ability to practice medicine. In areas where science cannot hold sway, however, neither can he. He is, understandably, too preoccupied to discern or intuit the impending disaster of the husband's suicide, which wipes away his temporary elation with being what Uncle George teasingly refers to as the "great man." It is hard not to see the husband's death, at least in part, as emblematic of the long-standing series of usurpations by the white man of the Indian's rights and wishes. In "The Doctor and the Doctor's Wife" it is the Indians who are bidden to do a job for the white man, and it is Dr. Adams who finally comes to feel that his home has been invaded and his authority usurped by a man of another race.

[5] While I think that Thomas Strychacz loses sight of the emergency nature of the doctor's mission and judges him too harshly in "Indian Camp," he has taken stock of important ironies and contrapuntal movements in these two stories, 61–65.

The doctor's status as a physician does not impress Dick Boulton, who, in fact, gets under Adams's skin by repeatedly calling him "Doc." Nor does being a man of medical science help him on the domestic front. His wife gives him credit neither for his judgment of Dick nor, as a Christian Scientist, for his medical knowledge. In his room the doctor notices his pile of unopened medical journals and is further irritated by its symbolic reminder that his expertise and authority are undermined in his own home. If the husband in "Indian Camp" has been wounded by an axe and kills himself because, as the doctor tells Nick, "he couldn't stand things," the doctor is metaphorically cut by the axe-wielding Indian Dick Boulton and then has his emotional wounds heavily salted by his wife. How much Dr. Adams can himself stand and for how long is open to question; but he has left his recently fondled and beloved shotgun in the corner of his room, shells scattered on his bed, and he has left the reader aware of the daily accumulation of humiliations that he has had to swallow and suspecting that when the gun is eventually put to use it might well be turned selfward by its owner.[6]

It would be a mistake to focus exclusively on the lessons that Nick learns in the first two stories, for his father occupies center stage in "The Doctor and the Doctor's Wife" and is of coequal importance in "Indian Camp." Any lessons that Nick learns in these stories are partial and only vaguely realized. From here on out, though, Nick is clearly the protagonist of his own stories, the next pair of which concern his painful awakening to the transitory nature of love. Depicting as it does the consequences of a loveless marriage for Nick's father, "The Doctor and the Doctor's Wife" corresponds to "The End of Something," where the teenaged Nick experiences for the first time how it feels when love dies.

While the story depicts a breakup and has at its emotional center the death of youthful love, the only actions described in detail are

[6] Readers who know of Dr. Hemingway's suicide a few years after the publication of this story and who know of Hemingway's own suicide may feel an eerie and retrospective poignancy at the appearance of the suicide theme so early in Hemingway's career and in stories that are highly autobiographical.

the rowing and fishing that Nick and Marjorie do. They have evidently fished together a good bit — indeed, fishing appears to be the focal point of their relationship — with Nick playing instructor to Marjorie. Marjorie seems to have little left to learn from Nick about fishing, showing herself quite capable in her handling of the rowboat and generally self-sufficient, which may well be part of the problem for Nick: he may feel threatened by her proficiency. It may be, as he implies, that having nothing left to teach her leaves him bored with their relationship. "You know everything. That's the trouble," he lashes out at her (34). As the couple sits down to a picnic dinner that Nick must force himself to eat, and as they watch an unromantic moonrise, Marjorie forces the issue, and Nick admits that he is no longer in love with her. "It isn't fun anymore," he tells her. "Not any of it" (34). With firmness and dignity, Marjorie does what Nick cannot bring himself to do: she takes command of the situation and rows away, leaving him to walk home.

The dialogue in the story is laconic even by Hemingway's standards; but it is fittingly so, reflecting teenage emotional confusion and its attendant inarticulate gracelessness. And although it is Marjorie who is rejected by Nick, it is also Marjorie who is depicted as the more decisive person, while Nick is shown lying down "with his face in the blanket . . . for a long time" (35). Although it was Nick who set out to end the relationship, as we learn from his conversations with his friend Bill, who shows up late in this story and again in the subsequent story, it is he who adopts the posture of the stunned victim.[7] "What's the matter, Nick?" Marjorie asks halfway through the story, sensing his tense moodiness. Nick's answer, "I don't know," is both truthful and evasive. Nick *feels* that he must break up with Marjorie but does not have her gumption and cannot speak openly. But it is also true that Nick cannot come to terms with why "something" must come to an end and why it must feel so deadening when it does. From an outsider's point of view, even

---

[7] Wendolyn Tetlow has drawn attention to the frequent recurrence of this sort of image, that of a man with his head bowed in *In Our Time*. It mirrors the sense of "loss and demoralization" that runs through the volume (59).

from the point of view of Nick's peer Bill, the breakup is just one of those youthful things. Bill, who was aware beforehand that Nick wanted to force a breakup, wastes no sympathy on Nick but, as the story winds down, calmly extracts a sandwich from the picnic basket that held no attraction for Nick.

Hemingway captures the pain and awkwardness of youth by steadfastly refusing to apply adjectives to either of the principal characters. The story's mood is revealed indirectly through extensive description of landscape and through reported action. Hemingway devotes his opening paragraphs — fully one-sixth of the story — to a description of the ghost town of Hortons Bay. The opening does not advance the plot in the least; and when the characters begin to do things, the action is slight and only obliquely related to the story's emotional center. A once-thriving lumber town, Hortons Bay serves less as a literal setting than as a metaphorical background for Nick and Marjorie's breakup. "There's our old ruin, Nick," says Marjorie, referring to the abandoned lakefront mill (32). Marjorie does not say these words, the first spoken in the story, with the intention of spinning a metaphor, for at this stage Nick has not revealed himself to be troubled, and she is engrossed in fishing. But as the story progresses, it becomes steadily more apparent that she is correct at a deeper level, for the ruins of the once-thriving town are Hemingway's objective correlative for the teenagers' ruined relationship. The town ran out of lumber, packed up, and moved on. Nick feels that his and Marjorie's love has somehow run out of "fun," and he leaves Marjorie to do the packing. For the third story in a row, a lakefront is the locus of pain and loss; and for the third story in a row, the protagonist is left floundering emotionally.

"The Three-Day Blow" depicts Nick in the aftermath of his breakup with Marjorie. The title refers to an autumn storm that is settling in while Nick and Bill spend the night in Bill's family cottage. At first Bill avoids mentioning the breakup; but he eventually broaches the topic, making clear his own opinion that the "Marge business" was doomed to failure because Marjorie was of a lower social class than Nick. Getting married, Bill says, leaves a man "absolutely bitched," for it means loss of freedom — a theme that will receive fuller treatment in a later Nick Adams story, "Cross-Country

Snow," and one that lies in the shadows cast by Dr. and Mrs. Adams's separate beds. But Nick has done especially well in this situation, Bill declares, because "you can't mix oil and water," and "now she can marry somebody of her own sort" (47). Nick answers with a sort of unemphatic agreement, assenting to his friend's words on the surface without demonstrating the least sign of emotional conviction that he has made a wise choice. The boys end their drinking bout with the resolution to go outside and do some hunting, so, once again, nature is the male's refuge from emotional turmoil, as it had been for the young Nick in "Indian Camp" and for Dr. Adams in "The Doctor and the Doctor's Wife": "Outside now the Marge business was no longer so tragic. It was not even very important. The wind blew everything like that away" (49).

By the end of the story, with the aid of the wind and, no doubt, of the whiskey they have drunk (an aid that has reasserted its power, for at one point Nick had felt sobered up), Nick indulges in a self-deception: he and Marjorie can always get back together. "He felt happy now. There was not anything that was irrevocable. . . . Nothing was finished. Nothing was ever lost" (48). Returning to once-meaningful places and recapturing former joys will become a familiar theme in Hemingway's work and will often be shown to be an attractive delusion, impossible to accomplish. Nick's false hope that "nothing was ever lost" is partly the product of his youth and partly an expression of the common desire to escape the necessity of facing the consequences of one's actions. In the next story, "The Battler," Nick will see how much truly can be lost to consequences.

While "The End of Something" employs imagery as its main technique, "The Three-Day Blow" depends on dialogue. Hemingway's ability to characterize through uncommented-on dialogue is already well developed in *In Our Time*. The tautness of his conversations, which quickly reached its apogee in *The Sun Also Rises* and his short stories of the 1920s and 1930s, shows itself to advantage in various ways in various stories; but in "The Three-Day Blow" Hemingway twice falls into the sort of narratorial intrusion that he ordinarily took pains to avoid. In one instance the narrator archly comments on the banality of the boys' conversation, directly telling the reader that the boys "sat looking into the fire and thinking of this profound truth" (44). Shortly afterwards the narrator remarks that "they were conducting the conversation on a high plane" (45). Hemingway's usual procedure would be, of course, to let the conversation stand on its own and to trust the reader to supply his or her own amused or sarcastic judgments. Small as they are in relation to the totality of the volume, the fact that these slips seem glaring gives evidence of the great care with which Hemingway crafted this first volume of stories and demonstrates how early in his career he had gained mastery of his particular brand of the modern show-don't-tell technique.

As the previous quotations indicate, there is room to debate the narrator's attitude toward Nick in this story — to what degree it is condescending and to what degree it is sympathetic — but its combination of humor and sympathy is unmistakable. No doubt Hemingway felt himself older and wiser than his protagonist and, therefore, able to make Nick an object of fun. On the other hand, Hemingway was still a young man when he wrote this story, and the real pain of early lost love would have been vivid to him, so the narrator's superior stance is tempered with poignancy. The pain of young love is a theme that is touched on elsewhere in *In Our Time* and is treated again in "Ten Indians," a story written shortly after the volume was published. While the short-story context is too slight, and the treatment of Nick here insufficiently weighty, to be called tragic, "The Three-Day Blow" anticipates the sort of romantic tragedies that would shortly catapult Hemingway to world fame. Underlying his great novels and many of his finest short stories is the belief that love is doomed. "If two people love each other there can be no happy end to it," he states categorically in *Death in the Afternoon* (122). Young as Nick still is here, essentially untragic as is his adolescent loss, his pain is not trivial, and he is beginning to learn that even the most important things in life — *especially* the most important things in life — are contingent and impermanent.

"The Battler" ends the first group of Nick Adams stories. Used as a replacement for the censored story "Up in Michigan," and thus the last story to be written for the volume, it was undoubtedly placed where it is by Hemingway to backfill a gap in his presentation of Nick's development. As Paul Smith has said, Hemingway "had in mind that interval between Nick's adolescence in 'The Three-Day Blow' and his maturity in the postwar narratives" to follow (120). Indeed, Nick himself makes much of his still being a "kid" at the story's outset, having just been sucker punched and thrown off a train by its brakeman. Walking along the railway through a woodsy swamp (a symbolic terrain that will be of vital importance when Nick returns to it in the volume's climactic story, "Big Two-Hearted River"), he comes upon a camp where he meets the ex-prize fighter Ad Francis and Ad's black fellow hobo and caretaker, Bugs. Ad takes a shine to Nick, and they talk. Nick notes the man's odd ways and listens to his boxing tales. But when Ad asks to borrow Nick's knife, Bugs tells Nick not to lend it to him. While they eat the supper that Bugs has cooked, it becomes apparent that Ad's attitude toward Nick has changed on account of the knife: Ad accuses Nick of being "snotty" and of butting in where he is not wanted and finally threatens to give him a beating. Bugs knocks Ad out with a blackjack, explaining to Nick that he must do so whenever Ad becomes too aggressive. To prevent a repetition of the incident, Bugs, maintaining his well-polished deference, asks Nick to move along before Ad comes to.

"The Battler" is the first story in which Nick is on his own, away from father, mother, and friends. He is "on the bum," making his own self-imposed, North American adolescent version of what Australian aborigines call "walkabout," self-testing, deliberately searching for experience. Temporarily adopting the role of the hobo (essentially Nick is an upper-middle-class teenager playing at hoboing) he encounters a real hobo. Venturing out under the common conception that experience leads to maturity and wisdom, Nick finds in Ad Francis someone for whom experience has meant ruin.

With his beaten, scarred face and missing ear, Ad is the walking embodiment of brutalized experience. Early in the story Nick thinks that experience will teach him, and thus help him avoid beatings. After having been socked in the eye and thrown from the train, he thinks that "he had fallen for it," but "they would never suck him in that way again" (53). But "the battler," whose very expertise was in boxing, clearly exemplifies that the experienced man may also take a beating from life. "I could take it," he says to Nick. "Don't you think I could take it, kid?" (55). But Ad's face is disfigured; his mood swings suddenly to uncalled-for aggression; and, ironically, his companion takes care of him by knocking him cold — all of which argues that in the end the boxer who survived because he could withstand the blows, the man who won his fights because of his "slow" heart, ended by succumbing to the series of events that life dished out to him. Indeed, utterly dependent on Bugs as he is, Ad is as close to infancy as he is to manhood.

When Nick first comes into the hobos' camp, Ad insists that the young man examine him closely. Nick, who has "a big bump coming up" over one eye, examines Ad's smashed-up face and takes his pulse, while Ad avers that his opponents used to "bust their hands" on him but that he had more stamina, outlasting his adversaries with his slow heart (53, 56). Though he is not conscious of the fact, Nick is, in effect, examining a potential future self, one that he must eventually learn to reject. The boxer, of course, lives by a stereotypically tougher-than-you, stronger-than-you, more potent-than-you macho code. It is clear, however, that the seemingly simple masculine code of the boxing ring served Ad quite poorly in the long run. Just as threat and bluster backfired when Nick's father threatened Dick Boulton, so Ad's strategy of rugged endurance has left him punch drunk and disfigured. Despite agreeing with Ad that "You got to be tough," Nick shows no signs of being a "battler" (55). He seems to want neither to dish it out nor to prove that he can "take it" when Ad threatens to knock his "can off" (59). Bugs has to save Nick in the moment of crisis by blackjacking Ad.

But the macho code of the boxer is only one side of Ad. He is not only punch drunk; he is also a man who has been irreparably harmed by a conflict between his public role and his private self. The other side of Ad shows that he not only battled in the ring but also battled his public, and perhaps himself, for this other side hints at an unconventional sexuality. When Nick asks what made Ad go crazy, Bugs relates the story of Ad's marriage to his female manager, who, for publicity reasons, he had previously said was his sister. Even though the incest was only apparent, the resulting negative public reaction drove away the "sister"/manager/wife and ended Ad's career. Now both men live off the money sent them by this "awful good-looking woman" who "looked enough like him to be his twin" (61). Bugs's use of the word *awful* lends a rich doubleness to his statement. Consciously, of course, he is using the word as American vernacular, as an intensifier equivalent to *very*. But he is also reflecting the public's opinion, perhaps his own unconscious opinion, and perhaps even that of Ad himself, by laying stress on the awfulness of sexual attraction to one's "sister," someone who looks just like oneself. Nick is free to consider, as is the reader, the difference between the simple version of the battler as boxer — the version demanded by the public — and the fuller, more private, more complicated, but equally defeated version that is revealed at the campfire.

"The Battler," then, is a version of an archetypal initiation story that Hemingway renders modern for "our time." The innocent protagonist is offered the experiences of life's veteran from which to learn. Yet Hemingway, as he does in all the young-Nick stories, withholds the center of narrative consciousness from Nick, leaving the reader to judge how fully the protagonist has absorbed the fittingly ironic postwar morals this story seems to point: fame brings not freedom but a straitjacket of expectations on the part of your public; the trajectory from champion to bum can be astonishingly rapid; the very source of your victories ("taking it") may turn out to be repeatedly enacted in defeat; that which is childish and that which is adult are not as separate as one first supposed; the various roles one wishes to play may conflict irreconcilably with the roles one is expected to play; experience may be of no value in the end. Frederic Henry will come to realize this last lesson in *A Farewell to Arms:* "You did not know what it was all about. You never had time to learn. They threw you in and told you the rules and the first time they caught you off base they killed you" — or wounded you (327). *Winner Take Nothing* Hemingway called his 1933 collection of short stories; and, while his own worldview is not ultimately as nihilistic as this stark title implies, his alter-ego Nick will learn through direct experience that comfort, security, love, meaning, sanity itself are utterly provisional.

Hemingway has taken Nick from boy to teenager in his first five stories, all of which seem to have the form of initiation narratives but none of which has a clearly defined and true epiphanic moment.[8] In "Indian Camp" Nick is too young, and the events that have transpired in the remote cabin are too bewildering to comprehend. At the story's end his retreat into false complacency about his own immortality is consistent with his youth. Experience has planted seeds, but they will lie dormant until maturity allows them to flower into insight. In "The Doctor and the Doctor's Wife" it is doubtful that Nick is even present to witness all the indignities borne by his father. From Nick's point of view the story should be taken as one that characterizes the household in which he has grown up. His response to his father is one of sympathetic intuition, as if he has watched this scene played out on a regular basis. There is an emotional landscape in the Adams household, and Nick is familiar with its prominent features. His father's emotional matrix of frustration and failure is palpable as he approaches Nick, who offers to lead the way in the soothing retreat to nature that typifies the endings of these stories.

The lesson of "The End of Something" is much clearer. The end of love feels like emotional death. But no sudden, keen insight occurs in response to this lesson. Rather, Nick's posture at the end of the story and his irritation with Bill, who may well have been the instigator of the breakup, reveal not an emotional resolve but a floundering that is replaced only by the callow self-deception of "The Three-Day Blow," where Nick manages to convince himself that consequences need not be faced and that one can always go back. Faced with a set of circumstances beyond his ability to endure, adolescent Nick comforts himself with a false notion in much the same way that young-boy Nick did at the end of "Indian Camp." Finally, in "The Battler" Nick is presented with experiences as strange and

---

[8] The epiphany is an important concept in the study of modernist fiction. Working by analogy from the term's original theological meaning, James Joyce defined the epiphany as an unexpected moment of sudden and intense enlightenment. His stories' emphasis on the contrast between the mundane turn of events that prompts the epiphany and its spiritual or quasi-spiritual nature has been dulled a great deal in subsequent critical practice. As we have seen, Hemingway was acquainted with Joyce and familiar with his work when he wrote *In Our Time*.

bewildering as those in "Indian Camp." This story, too, ends with Nick walking into the woods, but this time alone, and the degree to which he has thought through this strange night's lessons remains to be seen. Once again, there is no epiphanic scene of clear enlightenment. Rather, the lesson presents itself in all its complications, to be mulled over and worked through. It may be fair, then, to see this first group of stories as being about Nick's initiation; but they are initiation stories of a particularly subtle and deliberately limited kind.[9] The significance of these incidents to Nick is never articulated but remains submerged, an effect not to be uncovered by the writer, but discovered by the reader.

Stories of War and Love

After portraying Nick in five consecutive stories, the volume shifts away from him. He is not present in any of the next six stories, though he could have been the protagonist in any of them. He shares important similarities with several main characters, especially the young man in "A Very Short Story" and Krebs in "Soldier's Home." So, despite his absence, the volume continues to follow the developmental path begun in the Nick Adams stories: it moves through the stages of late adolescence and early adulthood, the stage at which Nick's progress is interrupted in "The Battler." When he next appears, in "Cross-Country Snow," he will be a young adult, probably married, and expecting to become a father. The six stories divide logically into two groups of three. The first group portrays somewhat younger characters and concentrates on the effects of war; the second group focuses on young-adult characters and concentrates on marital strife and unwanted pregnancy.

---

[9] Earl Rovit and Gerry Brenner have proposed the term "epistemological story" in place of "initiation story" to describe certain Hemingway fictions. Their phrase "emphasizes the learning process per se" instead of proving or even merely implying that a definite rite of passage has been achieved or a particular set of lessons conclusively learned by a protagonist (78). While the phrase has a degree of imprecision, so do Hemingway's young-Nick stories, and I think that their concept ultimately corresponds better to the fictions at hand than does the term "initiation story."

The core themes of loss, diminishment, and limitation introduced in the Nick Adams stories retain their centrality in the non-Nick stories. Likewise, confusion and pain continue to typify the emotional states of the protagonist. In the stories of young Nick Adams that we have just examined, culminating in "The Battler," two alternatives surface: either Nick is not himself the focus of the greatest suffering in the story, or, if he does suffer, he ends the story by denying his suffering. Nick's growth will be registered in the volume's final story, "Big Two-Hearted River," wherein he will take conscious, active steps to alleviate his suffering. In the intervening stories the main characters have become sufficiently mature to act on their own behalf if they are given meaningful alternatives (which are not always provided in Hemingway's world) and if they are able to muster the psychic energy to do so. The responses range from Krebs's passivity in "Soldier's Home" through the Revolutionist's perhaps willful self-delusion in the story of that name to the American wife's desperate quest for a satisfying direction for her life in "Cat in the Rain." Two things remain constant in the next six stories: the world is hard, and the forgetfulness and disregard of youth will no longer provide the anodyne that they did for young Nick. Now characters will come up square against harsh facts, and consequences will have to be faced. It is the World War that serves as the focal point for this important turn in the volume.

The war changes Nick himself in "Chapter VI," the vignette immediately following "The Battler," when he is wounded by machine-gun fire on the Italian front. "You and me we've made a separate peace," he tells his wounded comrade, Rinaldi (63). This briefly narrated incident marks the turning point in Nick's reaction to his experiences and simultaneously marks the turning point of the volume toward adult responses to pain and loss. "Soldier's Home" and "The Revolutionist" demonstrate that this shift is not absolute; but, while characters may still exhibit the urge to deny or repress, withdrawal and psychic evasion of the truth will no longer yield satisfactory results. When we return to Nick's chronicle, he will no longer attempt such evasions. He will no longer be a child curled up in his father's arms, and it will no longer be possible for him to pretend that his problems will go away. Willy-nilly he will have joined ranks with the Indian husband and wife, with his father, with Ad Francis — with all those he has witnessed suffering deeply. In the meantime, other characters are shown losing in love and losing in war, as the volume plays variations on the theme of hard experience "in our time."

Prior to "A Very Short Story," the vignettes carried the load of specifically modern substance that the book's title betokens. The first Nick stories do not depend on any particularly twentieth-century set of circumstances, but are built on timeless themes and story lines. However, beginning with "A Very Short Story," the stories themselves become more closely linked to modern particularities. Indeed, two of the three (this story and "The Revolutionist") were originally published among the eighteen vignettes of *in our time*, Hemingway's virtuoso exercise book in modernism.

"A Very Short Story" is a brief description of an unnamed soldier who falls in love with his nurse while hospitalized in Italy. Although the soldier is not called Nick, and Hemingway composed the story before he had written any of the Nick Adams pieces, it is noteworthy that the events of the story jibe closely with those of the Nick-Rinaldi vignette that immediately precedes it. It should also be noted that Hemingway chose to include this piece in the fuller context of *In Our Time,* chose to shift its status from vignette to story, and chose to place it where it is in the volume. This set of choices complements the intentions he had when he composed the piece. Whether or not the story is literally about Nick Adams, then, cannot be proven, but its thematic resonance with Nick's development is beyond dispute. The unnamed ex-soldier's love affair seems to have been his particular version of a "separate peace" in the midst of war, for he is crushed when he receives a Dear John letter from Luz after his return to the United States. She writes that "theirs had been only a boy and girl affair" and not true love (66). Luz, who remained in Italy, gets dumped in her turn in a passage that mocks her own naivete, and the story ends with the protagonist contracting gonorrhea during a taxicab tryst with a Chicago shop assistant.

A strictly biographical approach cannot resolve all issues, even with a writer as autobiographical as Hemingway. Nonetheless, it is impossible to ignore the highly autobiographical quality of "A Very

Short Story," which serves as a sort of résumé of Hemingway's relationship with Agnes von Kurowsky.[10] Indeed, in the first published version of the story the nurse's name is Ag, and the Italian place names correspond to those traveled by Kurowsky in her tour as a Red Cross nurse. The two noteworthy departures from autobiography into purely imagined fiction relate to the sexual dimensions of the story. Despite what some biographers have claimed, and despite the wishful thinking of some Hemingway "fans," it is highly unlikely that Hemingway and Kurowsky had sex in his hospital bed. The sex in the story is a wholly fictional creation (as is the venereal disease contracted by the young veteran), but rather than being a merely self-indulgent wish fulfillment, this first "created" aspect of the story is included to set up the story's second wholly fictional aspect: the final paragraph.

While the story might be criticized for its atypically direct presentation and for insufficient authorial distancing, one crucial aspect is left open to interpretation. Hemingway was devastated by Kurowsky's rejection, but this fact proves nothing about the reaction of the young man in the story. Hemingway's narrator tells us only what he does, not what he thinks, and his response to Luz's rejection remains ambiguous. The young man's sexual encounter in the taxicab could have been prompted by a misguided attempt to revenge himself on Luz. Those who see the story as a bit of Hemingway bravado will favor this possibility; but again, biography, while relevant, proves nothing. The encounter could be an attempt to assuage his hurt and loneliness, to find a replacement for Luz, or simply to seek sexual relief. It might be seen as a modern response to an age-old form of wounding: there have always been young men who were deceived by

---

[10] The fullest description of Hemingway's hospitalization and his relationship with Kurowsky is to be found in Villard and Nagel's *Hemingway in Love and War*. Readers of *A Farewell to Arms* will also note that this story and the preceding Nick-Rinaldi vignette contain several narrative and thematic germs that are elaborated in that novel. Those interested in Hemingway's involvement in World War I may also consult Michael Reynolds's *Hemingway's First War*, which remains valuable even though it has been superseded in some respects by Villard and Nagel's study.

love, but the availability of the virtually anonymous shop girl and the convenience of the taxicab are particularly modern. His response could have been a combination of these various elements. There can be no certainty on the subject, since the narrator never reveals the man's thoughts. The reader knows merely that the soldier never wrote back to Luz (feigned indifference designed to send a who-cares message? stunned and humiliated anguish?) and that, as the story flatly states, "a short time after he contracted gonorrhea from a sales girl in a loop department store while riding in a taxicab through Lincoln Park" (66). In a story that stresses the transience of love, in a story where both principal characters are made to look gullible, or at least vulnerable, this meaningless tryst, whether indulged in for vengeance or out of sorrow or need, exacts a high price. The soldier is tricked by love and then by sex, and all is narrated with a frankness that was calculated to announce that the author was familiar with the ways of the modern world. Many a resident of Hemingway's Oak Park, not knowing a thing about the autobiographical dimensions of the story, would nonetheless have found it shocking. Characters and readers alike are disabused of romantic notions of love and marriage and a baby carriage.[11]

From the heartbreak and disease of "A Very Short Story" the volume moves to one of its most important stories, "Soldier's Home," which continues the chronicles of modern soldiering and repeats the focus on homecoming. Harold Krebs is subject to a more figurative, but nonetheless real, disease. If "A Very Short Story" is one of the slighter works in the collection, and its dramatization is not entirely satisfactory, "Soldier's Home" presents itself as an early tour de force of show-don't-tell suggestiveness. Here the author's experiments with repetition and sentence patterning are used to advantage, as is his growing skill in the construction of dialogue. Once again, while "Soldier's Home" is not a Nick Adams story, what we

---

[11] Pursuing the biographical dimensions of the story, Milton Cohen has stressed the young Hemingway's keen desire to deal with the sort of raw truths that would reject the typical Oak Park view of the world. Hemingway was surely aware that in doing so he would be providing a shock to his prudish parents.

know of Nick's wounding and what we will later see of his postwar struggles make this story consistent with Nick's development. Insofar as Harold and Nick are at the same stage of life and share important characteristics, and insofar as this story is exemplary of the experience of many a returning veteran of the First World War, this could well be Nick's story too. Surely he would be sympathetic to its protagonist's problems.

Harold Krebs has returned to his small Oklahoma town significantly later than his fellow hometown veterans. He quickly finds that no one is interested in listening to even the grisliest war stories, and only ex-soldiers care to exchange views on what the war was really like. Krebs has withdrawn into an inactive life, where his greatest satisfactions come from watching and reading rather than doing. His parents are disappointed that he is not taking the customary steps toward career and marriage with the desired briskness of spirit, and his mother confronts him directly on the subject of getting started with his adult life. Harold, however, wants nothing to do with jobs, nothing to do with marriage, and nothing to do with his mother. He tells her that he does not love her but retracts the statement immediately, not because it is false but because his life will go more smoothly if he can cut the awkward incident as short as possible. Krebs's one goal since returning from the war has been to eliminate complications and "consequences," but it becomes increasingly apparent that doing so constitutes a refusal to become involved with ordinary adult activities and relationships. Exactly what happened to Krebs in the war is not clear — perhaps that is the intentionally submerged part of this story's iceberg — but something in his experiences has depressed him deeply. The tragedy is that he is too weakened to help in his own recovery, and no one else seems to care.

Krebs was greeted by a callous and blasé hometown and by parents who want him to conform to the predictable and stultifying prewar pattern of life as if nothing had transpired in Europe. Powerless to claim sincere attention, he is unable to readjust to life in small-town Oklahoma. Krebs is seemingly faced with two alternatives: he may live the life that is scripted for him by mother, father, and townsfolk; or he may forge a new life more consistent with his now modernized experience, a life symbolized by the option of moving to Kansas City. The first option is impossible, for he has changed too much while away in the war. He is no longer religious; he is now sexually experienced (in one type of sexual encounter, the quick, simple, and temporary wartime liaison); and his closed-in, small-minded hometown offers nothing capable of engaging his energy. But since he does not have the strength to forge a postwar life for himself, by default he falls into a childish state of withdrawal and developmental paralysis. The story forces one to question the resolution he makes in the final paragraph to go to Kansas City. While this would seem to be a positive choice — really the only life-affirming option available to him — the story has given no sign that Krebs has the strength to carry out this plan. All signs point to the contrary. Just as he pretends to love his mother and to be religious in order to get through an unpleasant moment as quickly and easily as possible, so, too, in a moment of easy self-deception he pretends to himself that he will move to Kansas City.

No one comes off well in this troubling story. The community is unwilling to honor its veterans by truly acknowledging their service. If acknowledgment means listening to a few lurid war stories that provide a bit of entertainment and do not challenge the listeners' preconceptions of the war, then fine. If acknowledgment means throwing a parade and partying for a few days, then also fine. But if acknowledgment means paying attention to what this first truly modern war was really like, that is something in which the community has no interest. Indeed, "people seemed to think it was rather ridiculous for Krebs to be getting back so late, years after the war was over" (69). It is the war-benumbed Krebs who studies the histories and maps of the war, not the public, which is depicted as content with its own ignorance, preferring titillating recruiting-poster mythology to a reality that would be at once more prosaic and more complicated than the received versions it wishes to file away, once and for all, as the established truth about the war. Krebs's hometown typifies the American 1920s isolationist response to the Great War. After ensuring itself that the cause was sacred, after mass mobilization, then demobilization in the first global war, the country wanted to forget its involvement as quickly as possible.

But it is not only Krebs's neighbors who are unwilling or unable to acknowledge the vast changes he has undergone but also — even more culpably — his parents. In the opening paragraphs we see that he has outgrown two identities: first he traded in the uniform of a Methodist college student for that of the Marines, then, during his extended postwar service on the Rhine, he had begun to outgrow his military uniform. What will his next uniform be? On his return from the war he receives no help in forging an adult identity. His father is "noncommittal" and apparently aloof. His mother "often came in when he was in bed and asked him to tell her about the war, but her attention always wandered" (70). A number of critics have painted Mrs. Krebs as a "bitch mother," and this characterization is accurate in that she bears responsibility for the callous aspects of her behavior. Unwilling to pay attention to her son's talk of the war, even when she solicits it, she is nonetheless prepared to guilt-trip him into compliance with her wishes: "Don't you love your mother, dear boy?" (75). It is also accurate to say, however, that, like Mrs. Adams of "The Doctor and the Doctor's Wife," she victimizes her family out of her own limitations. Hers is the tyranny of pious senti-mentality and predictable moralizing, and her chief verbal weapon is the cliché: "We are all of us in His [God's] Kingdom. . . . Boys like Charley Simmons are on their way to being really a credit to the community. . . . All work is honorable" (75). All of this is said to her son, whose first adult work had consisted of participating in every major U.S. engagement in the Great War. Expressing no concern that Harold could have been wounded or killed, nor any relief that he has returned in one piece, she instead makes evident to her son that her primary preoccupation is that he may have lost his virginity. To his openly apparent psychic distress she has no response, and probably little awareness. Harold quickly withdraws his truly fright-ening revelation that "I don't love anybody" because he knows it is beyond the ken of his premodern mother, whose grand gesture to-ward acknowledging the new generation is to join his father in of-fering Harold the use of the family car "to take some of the nice girls out riding" (76, 75).

For his part, the weary and passive Krebs will never push the is-sue, even when he has a need to do so. Telling the truth versus tell-

ing lies is one of the story's important motifs, and ultimately Krebs
learns to choose between truth and falsehood on the basis of emotional convenience rather than out of moral principle. Lying about
the war makes him feel nauseated, and this effect prompts him to
stop lying about it. On the other hand, it is too difficult to tell his
mother the truth about his lack of religious feeling or about his inadequate plans for a career or adult life, so he lies to her. He wants
no scenes and no complications. There are lies both of commission
and of omission: not only will he fib; he will also avoid openly airing
his feelings. He will stifle his rightful desire to have his new status acknowledged, preferring to let his mother baby him and his father
remain aloof. If they do not want to hear about the war, then he will
not make them do so. He will evade his father's directive for a
meeting. Even when the stakes are as tempting as the pretty girls in
town, he will not make the effort to play the necessary social game.

"Soldier's Home" is a tour de force of irony. Whether the word
Soldier's is interpreted as a contraction or as a possessive, the title
must be taken ironically, for Krebs's home is no place for an ex-
soldier. That he is not at home is readily apparent not only in his
interactions with his mother but also in his attitude to women. Although Krebs has been psychically damaged by his military experience, the chaotic, mechanized, fully modernized war was actually
simpler than life back home proves to be. With women in Europe
"there was not all this talking. You couldn't talk much and you did
not need to talk. It was simple and you were friends" (72). But back
home the girls live in "a complicated world of already defined alliances and shifting feuds," and Krebs does "not want to get into the
intrigue and the politics" (71). And although he likes to look at the
pretty girls and finds the "pattern" that they make "exciting," he
had not wanted to come home from Germany and its simple set of
rules in the first place.

Feuds, alliances, intrigue, and *politics* are words better suited to a
description of the war than to pleasant or healthy interpersonal relationships. While Krebs may eventually be able, by reading his books
and maps, to make sense of the military and political terrain he
passed through, he studiously avoids summoning up the psychic energy required to enter the sexual arena. To do so would require him

to communicate, and this he cannot do. Nor can anyone else, for there is not an instance of honest communication in the entire story outside of Krebs's remembered transactions with prostitutes. Krebs, like Nick in "The Three-Day Blow," wants to play the game of love without having to face any consequences. Nick's belief that "nothing was finished. Nothing was ever lost" is understandable in light of his youth (48). Much more troublingly, the war-traumatized, mother-plagued Krebs wants to conduct his entire life on the principle of no consequences, a strategy that is untenable for an adult.[12]

Whether Krebs will recover himself in Kansas City (if, indeed, he goes there at all) must remain a matter of speculation, but it seems safe to say that any recovery he may make will not be swift. Krebs's war talk, and particularly the "unimportant lies" that he told, finally result in his "losing" the war rather than coming to terms with it. Whether exaggerating to his reluctant hometown audience or talking as an old soldier to other old soldiers, the upshot of all the talk is nullification: "In this way he lost everything," the narrator concludes (70). Krebs's response is a retreat into a search for the simple and the predictable. His desire for patterns and his willingness to watch his younger sister play indoor baseball betoken a desire for order and for rules, but only the sort of rules that refer to themselves and are thus kept out of the messy world of consequences. Krebs does not want girls themselves; he likes to contemplate the patterns they make. What he really hopes for in his war studies are plenty of good maps. Maps schematize and simplify the complicated mess of warfare that Krebs knew at first hand, boiling it down to a few simple lines on paper — that is, to patterns. But patterns are not the same as the day-to-day reality of war, nor are patterns of love a substitute for the real thing.[13] Unfortunately for him, Krebs is interested in patterns not as a preparation for or guide to reentering life but as a means of withdrawing further from it.

---

[12] I am indebted to Tateo Imamura for noting the political terms used in relation to love interests outlined above (105).

[13] Robert W. Lewis has written about Krebs's attraction to patterns and his decision in the final paragraph to go watch his sister play indoor baseball.

"The Revolutionist" is of a piece with the two preceding stories in that it provides another variation on the theme of postwar alienation and upheaval. Like "A Very Short Story" it was originally published as one of the vignettes of *in our time,* and like many of those vignettes it is thoroughly rooted in the particulars of the postwar world. The vignette that precedes it ("Chapter VIII") embodies the anti-immigrant feeling of the 1920s and also includes a Hungarian character, thus providing an interesting counterpoint to "The Revolutionist." While the story line is short and simple — indeed, it is no more than a sketch — no story in the volume has more deeply embedded historical and political allusions.[14] One of only two stories narrated in the first person, it points at the gap between the narrator and the young Magyar "revolutionist" of the title, who travels around Europe penniless on behalf of the Communist Party. He has worked for the Red Hungarian Soviet and subsequently suffered at the hands of Miklós von Horthy's successful counterrevolutionary White forces.

The young man's precarious existence; his wandering homelessness; his torture, exile, and imprisonment for a political party; his faith in communism — all of these elements make the story a valuable snapshot of the European years immediately succeeding the Great War. But the collision of the nonpolitical with the political renders the piece something more than a snapshot. The young man loves nature: "He was very eager to walk over the pass while the weather held good. He loved the mountains in the autumn" (82). He was delighted with Italy not just because of his naive belief in its communist future but also because "it was a beautiful country" (81). He also loves art. So although he cannot afford to buy food and must bum train rides from fellow-traveling conductors, he uses what little money he does have to buy reproductions of the Italian mas-

---

[14] Although their various interpretations differ from one another and are not consistently of a piece with the interpretation I have given here, three articles can be recommended to the reader in search of background information on the particularities of postwar Hungarian politics and the works of art referred to in the story. See the entries in the bibliography for Groseclose, Hunt, and Johnston.

ters. His idealism motivates him to exchange the beauty of nature
and art for the false promise of political revolution and party aspira-
tion. In a sad symbol of his ill-advised dedication to ideology over
aesthetics, he keeps his precious art reproductions hidden inside his
copy of the Communist Party magazine.

Perhaps the young man is unable to learn from experience. It is
not clear whether his refusal to admit the painful inferences to be
drawn from his experiences is the result of some profound inner
wounding or of some stubborn strain of naivete. Either way, and
unlike the narrator, he continues to profess faith in the ability of political movements to make things better, to make life more beautiful.
The narrator, significantly, chooses not to reply to the young man's
seemingly blithe expressions of optimism in the Italian Communist
movement. "You have everything here," he says. "It is the one
country that everyone is sure of" (81). The narrator's purposeful si-
lence reveals that he knows that he is working for a lost cause. In
contrast, the young man has been tortured in his own country; yet,
he continues to express great optimism, echoing the party-line cant.

Although the narrator is wiser than the revolutionist, the fact that
he does not try to enlighten the latter does not necessarily bespeak
callousness or cynicism. The narrator may feel that some cause, even
a hopeless one, is better than no cause; after all, he himself keeps
working for the party. When one is committed to a cause, when
one's sense of self has become tied to it, turning back or admitting
wrong can exact too high an emotional price. At any rate, the young
man's zeal, that of the true believer, does not admit even the strongest evidence in contradiction to his beliefs: "In spite of Hungary, he
believed altogether in the world revolution" (81). Alternatively, the
narrator may feel that the beating administered to the revolutionist
has rendered him too shaky to benefit from any lessons in skepticism
that the narrator might offer. A tragedy of the times, then: a young
man suited for appreciating the real beauties of nature and art is
moved by a combination of temperament and circumstances into
chasing an unrealizable vision of social beauty falsely proffered by
utopian politics.

The story indirectly and allusively pushes the reader in the direction of seeing the revolutionist as a Christ figure. Of all the painters,

"Mantegna he did not like" (81). Mantegna's *The Dead Christ* (housed in Milan, where Hemingway was hospitalized in 1918) depicts Christ's agony and his tortured body. The painting includes the word *dead* in its title. It is a painting of Christ as corpse, containing no hint of his eventual triumph over death. It is understandable that someone recently tortured for his efforts to "save" his country might not want to look at this deadest depiction of the dead Savior. The revolutionist's imprisonment in Sion (with its play on Zion, the heavenly city of God) ends the story on a bleak and ironic note. After the war, faith in causes is utterly suspect, and Christ's story — Western culture's central salvation narrative — becomes the stuff of modernist irony.

Love, Marriage, No Babies: Four Stories

The next four stories concern the problems of postwar American expatriate newlyweds. The stories' thematic nexus consists of several interrelated topics: European travel, marital discord, sexual difficulties, and anxieties related to pregnancy and impending parenthood. "Mr. and Mrs. Elliot" is the first of three consecutive non-Nick stories, and the quartet ends with "Cross-Country Snow," which resumes Nick's narrative after a six-story hiatus.

"Mr. and Mrs. Elliot," the most openly satirical work in the volume, pokes fun at elements of expatriate life for which Hemingway had little sympathy. Hubert Elliot is a man without much to recommend him. Sexually timid, impotent on his wedding night and probably later (at least intermittently), he had "wanted to keep himself pure prior to marriage so that he could bring his wife the same purity of mind and body that he expected of her" (85). Humorously, this bit of leftover Victorian sexual moralism wins no favor with girls, to whom he always confides his pure intentions, for "nearly all the girls lost interest in him" after he explains his feelings (85). He marries Cornelia, a Southern woman fifteen years his senior with a delicate constitution. Her bedroom encounters with Mr. Elliot apparently bring her little satisfaction, so, although "they wanted a baby more than anything else in the world," they have sex with an infrequency that is surprising in view of all the "saving up" each of them had done before their marriage (87). By the end of the story Mrs. Elliot is in an openly lesbian relationship with a girlfriend of long standing in "the big mediaeval bed" in the Elliots' rented chateau. In contrast to her bedroom behavior with Hubert, with whom Cornelia "could not attempt it very often," she and her girlfriend "had many a good cry together," the narrator euphemistically explains (87, 88). Meanwhile, Hubert seems content with the girlfriend's presence since she is a much better typist of his poetry than his wife is. The story implies that he is quite willing to sublimate his sexual energy into the writing of long but worthless poems, since he spends all night writing them while his wife is in bed with his newfound typist.

As if it were not bad enough to be a sexual failure, Hubert is also a bad writer who pays a vanity publisher to bring out the long poems he writes so terribly quickly. Worst of all, he takes his bad poetry seriously. His sexual incapacity is not his original sin but the badge of shame assigned to him by Hemingway as a punishment for the sin of being a fake. Hubert's bad poetry and his contentment with playing the rich American tourist comprise his worst failures. Indeed, the Elliots' whole crowd smacks of overprivileged dilettantism. The circle of friends retains a false sense of superiority: "They all sat around the Café du dome, avoiding the Rotonde across the street because it is always so full of foreigners" (87). They attend universities merely to be able to say that they have done so. They collect place names for later name-dropping and confine their experience of Europe to the safe, comfortable, and perfectly predictable habits and haunts of the wealthy abroad. They will return home essentially untouched, secure in their illusion that they have experienced Europe; but the story exists to set them straight, showing their experiences to be as sham as Hubert's poetry and marriage. Hubert remains oblivious to all. He cannot grasp that his prudery is the product of another time; he cannot grasp that his poetry is worthless; he cannot grasp the implications of the fact that, after manipulating him into marriage, his wife is more content with another woman than with him.

It would seem that Cornelia has married Hubert to gain the cover of respectability, to have a baby, and, perhaps, to explore bisexual inclinations. I say *perhaps* because, although there is evidence for the last possibility, it remains particularly open to speculation.

On the one hand, the story provides several signs that the women have had a relationship before the never-named girlfriend's arrival in France, suggesting that the marriage was a setup on Cornelia's part. When the girlfriend arrives in France, Cornelia calls her "Honey," and on her arrival "Mrs. Elliot became much brighter" (87). Hubert's mother cries when she meets Cornelia, which can imply that Hubert is a mama's boy; that she is disappointed in Cornelia's looks, age, or station in life; or that she is horrified at her son's having married someone who gives every indication of not being heterosexual. On the other hand, there is evidence that Cornelia wants — or temporarily makes herself believe that she wants — a heterosexual relationship. She exhibits excitement over Hubert's courtship kisses, and Hemingway puns that "sometimes when they had been kissing together a long time, Cornelia would ask him to tell her again that he had kept himself really straight for her" (86). While Cornelia may be feigning excitement, in such a satiric story the pun about Hubert's erection is more likely aimed at skewering her own inexperienced lust. So it may be that she is desirous of adding a heterosexual component to her love life, or it may be that she only wants a baby and the cover of marriage; but either way, Hubert leaves her sexually disappointed and babyless. Either way, his gullibility and sexual ignorance appear to be boundless: "He could never remember just when it was decided that they were to be married. But they were married" (86).

Finally, the story is remarkable for its narrative voice, unusual in the Hemingway canon. The distancing and purposeful neutrality of Hemingway's previous narrators give way to a narrator with an overtly satirical agenda. His tone ranges from slyly humorous to openly snide and reveals a consistently superior stance heretofore seen only in a few short passages. While expatriate dilettantes are a worthy target for ridicule, one cannot help but feel that this story was too easy for a writer of Hemingway's talents. With more complexity, more sympathy, and more depth, he would return to the theme of expatriate life in works such as *The Sun Also Rises*. The humorous vein and witty touches compensate the reader but do not elevate the story to the status of the volume's better works, for it circumvents Hemingway's strongest suit: his ability to create fictions that achieve richness because of their suggestiveness and allusiveness. While ambiguities remain in "Mr. and Mrs. Elliot," they are not of the order, depth, or magnitude of those in his finest work.

"Cat in the Rain" also centers on a newlywed couple traveling in Europe and, once again, depicts a dissatisfied wife. Here, however, the action is dramatized in more typical Hemingway fashion. Although it does not quite reach the quality of fine-tuned evocation achieved in the descriptive opening of "The End of Something," the story's first paragraph likewise evokes a mood and indirectly describes a troubled relationship. This time it is the woman who is unhappy with the staleness of the relationship. Written with the trademark repetitions and rhythms of Hemingway's 1920s style, the first paragraph describes a rainy day in an Italian seaside hotel. The husband is lying on the bed, reading; the wife is bored and lonely and apparently desirous of a domestic life that is at once richer and more routine. At first she focuses her attention on a cat she sees outside the window, sheltering itself from the rain under a café table. Her attempt to catch the cat might seem at first to be merely something she has invented to break the monotony of the day, but it becomes clear that she has placed an extraordinary importance on obtaining the animal. "Oh, I wanted it so much. I wanted a kitty," she says after her failed attempt to rescue it (92).

Preoccupied with his reading, not putting the bed to the use his wife would apparently prefer, George does not immediately sense the profundity of his wife's dissatisfaction. Instead, the hotel owner displays this sort of intuitive intelligence, and makes "something [feel] very small and tight inside the girl" (93). The man orders the cat fetched and taken up to the couple's room to be presented to the yearning woman. But what does she yearn for? The cat embodies her desire for sensual pleasure: "I want to have a kitty to sit on my lap and purr when I stroke her" (93). Looking into a mirror, she expresses her desire to let her hair grow long, which succeeds in temporarily attracting George's attention, and then, in an outburst of "I wants," she makes clear her desire for a traditional house, which she does not have in the wandering expatriate life or extended honeymoon in which they are now engaged. These desires for traditional feminine and domestic trappings recurrently attach to the cat, which becomes a symbol of her unsatisfied longings. That the end point of these desires is probably the wish to have a baby is reinforced by the story's culminating image of the maid, who has been sent by the hotel owner, holding the cat like a baby "pressed tight against her and swung down against her body" (94). The momentary callousness George exhibits in ignoring his wife's frustration — "Oh, shut up and get something to read," he says (94) — seems to reveal a habitual insensitivity and indifference on his part. There is nothing in the story to suggest that the hotel owner is a literal rival of George's, but he should be seen as a counterpoint to George's immaturity and self-centeredness. Suggestively, the hotel owner is referred to as "the padrone," which in Italian means "father" — a maker of babies — and, unlike George, he "want[s] to serve" the unhappy woman (92).

Not ready to settle down, George prefers his wife with her boyish haircut and without a baby. Her petulant manner does little to serve what are essentially expressions of her understandable desire for a more settled and mature identity. They will gain her nothing from George. In "Out of Season," however, a similar disagreement between another American couple traveling in Italy takes on darker tones. Here, instead of indulging in seemingly petulant outbursts the wife has developed a colder, deeper, more calculated anger, and although the story contains humor, a deep division between husband and wife is apparent. What is not apparent is the source of their discord. These two stories join "The Doctor and the Doctor's Wife" as studies in the failure of communication between spouses. It is a theme to which Hemingway returns in future stories, perhaps most brilliantly in "Hills Like White Elephants" (1927).

From the outset of "Out of Season" Tiny, the wife, attempts to keep her distance both literally and figuratively from her husband and Peduzzi, the drunken guide who is about to take them on an illegal off-season trout-fishing trip; it is clear that she does not want to be on this excursion. She and her husband (he is never named) have quarreled at lunch. The trio's walk through town under the disapproving eyes of the townspeople is a dark comedy of errors and miscommunication. Peduzzi, ever concerned not to allow his drunkenness to die out on him, stops to buy marsala — only to find that the store is closed. The three walk on to the inaptly named

Concordia, where, much to the amusement of the girl who waits on them, the husband buys the marsala and tries to patch things up with his wife. They continue their journey, Peduzzi taking ever more liberties with his employers, Tiny still fuming and resentful, and the husband wishing that he had never come but unable to make himself call the trip off. Finally, just as they reach a spot on the river that is suitable for fishing, Tiny turns back, for, in one more instance of miscommunication, the couple mistakenly believes that they must continue on farther. When Peduzzi discovers that he and the husband have no lead to weight the fishing lines, the husband seizes the opportunity to call off the trip, pays Peduzzi what will undoubtedly turn out to be more drinking money, and fobs him off by arranging "probably" to meet the following morning — an appointment that the husband has no intention of keeping.

This outline of the story's events cannot, of course, do complete justice either to the series of comic errors embedded in it or to the much more troubling but submerged aspects that almost surface on several occasions. The story seems to have a comic, if not entirely happy, ending: Peduzzi is content to have played the ingratiating guide and been paid more money than he has rightly earned; Tiny has returned to the hotel, out of the cold wind and away from the two irritating men; the husband has wiggled out of the ill-advised engagement of Peduzzi as a guide; and no one has been arrested for out-of-season fishing. The sun even comes out. But there is the matter of the marital quarrel, which remains unresolved. Tiny's dark response to her husband that "None of it makes any difference," a remark out of proportion to anything disclosed in the story, remains particularly troubling and enigmatic (99).

There are clues to the mystery, however. The source of the quarrel seems to be that the wife is pregnant. Whether or not she initially desired the pregnancy is uncertain, but now Tiny wants to keep the child. Her husband does not, and his suggestion that the couple go fishing out of season (break the law) is akin to asking her to seek an abortion in a Catholic country. She wants no part of either "operation" and resents her husband's attempts to coerce her. To declare that a reckless fishing trip masks a marital quarrel over abortion is to plunge deep in pursuit of the iceberg's submarine bulk, but there is substantial evidence to support the reading. Biographically inclined critics have pointed to the story's period of composition, which co-incided with Hemingway's difficulty in coming to terms with his first wife, Hadley's, pregnancy. That Hemingway felt trapped by the im-pending responsibilities of fatherhood is certain; that he suggested an abortion and that she resisted is quite likely. This is the bio-graphical context that informs not only "Out of Season" but also "Cat in the Rain," "Cross-Country Snow," and the justly famous "Hills Like White Elephants."[15]

While suggestive of the story's germ, this biographical informa-tion cannot stand as decisive textual evidence. For that, there is the story's placement in the volume, the figurative import of the action, and the allusive imagery. First, the story is placed in the midst of a quartet of marital-trouble stories, all of which treat the question of having babies. Specifically, it is sandwiched between "Cat in the Rain," where the wife wants to conceive a baby and the husband does not, and "Cross-Country Snow," where the wife is pregnant and the husband ruefully contemplates the end of his freedom-filled wanderyears as an inevitable fact. Both intuition and logic suggest that "Out of Season" treats the intermediate position, between a pregnancy not desired by the husband and a baby on the way.

Furthermore, the story's imagery supports the idea of abortion as the source of conflict.[16] The springtime setting in Italy is full of im-plication: spring is the season of rebirth, and Italy is a Catholic country, where abortion would be viewed with disapproval. Spring fishing is illegal because it is spawning season, and the young trout must be given the chance to be born. To take the adults is poten-tially to destroy the young, an act that would be self-defeating for fishermen, is illegal, and is also immoral since it runs counter to na-ture's design. Thus the severe disapproval of the townspeople who

---

[15] See Kenneth S. Lynn's *Hemingway* (1987) for a biographical reading along these lines (199–204, 249–253, 363–364).

[16] Kenneth G. Johnston was the first to suggest that the couple is quarrel-ing over the man's suggestion that Tiny have an abortion. My reading of the story's imagery is indebted to him. See "'Out of Season': The Tip of the Iceberg," in his *The Tip of the Iceberg* (1987), especially pages 32–34.

stare down at the trio as they walk along; the town beggar is the only one who returns Peduzzi's elaborate greetings. The young husband's guilt and anxiety are apparent: "Everybody in the town saw us going through with these rods. We're probably being followed by the game police now. I wish we weren't in on this damn thing" (100). Reading doubly, one sees that the guilt reflects his realization that his wife is right and he is wrong: fishing out of season is a contravention of nature, and so is abortion. As he sits down on the riverbank to fish, he seems to feel the whole moral weight of the Catholic town looming over him: "He could see the houses of the town and the campanile over the edge of the hill" (101). Thus his great relief when he is given the opportunity to cut short the unwise expedition because the fishing weights have been forgotten.

The river is the story's symbolic focus. At this time of year, when its natural rhythms are allowed to run their course, it is the place of renewal. When it is interfered with out of season, it becomes the locus of wrongdoing and guilt. Thus, when the despised Peduzzi arrives at the fishing site, he stands "gesturing at the river. It was brown and muddy. Off on the right there was a dump heap" (100). This imagery is consistent with a hallmark of modernist writing, the wasteland imagery employed most famously by T. S. Eliot. It is a metaphor for the moral swamp toward which the husband has urged himself and Tiny. Tiny, who never wanted to go to the river in the first place, yields to her husband's insistence and goes; but once in sight of it, she turns back. That her husband urges her to do so reveals his own change of heart. In a misguided effort to save face ("Of course you haven't got the guts to just go back," she tells him [100]) he will unhappily persevere with what he has committed himself to do, then seize the opportunity of reprieve given by the absence of the weights. After deciding not to fish, "the young gentleman felt relieved" (102). Even the weather changes symbolically: at the outset a chilly wind is blowing, and the day alternates between clouds and sun, paralleling the alternatives of abortion or birth that divide the couple; but as soon as the husband is certain that he is not going to break the law, "the sun came out. It was warm and pleasant" (102).

If there is a villain in the piece, it is not the inept and drunken Peduzzi but the husband, whom, as Kenneth S. Lynn has noted, the author has kept at arm's length by constantly using the stilted appellation "the young gentleman" (202). Having insisted on the illegal trip, he proceeds merely to drift through it, neither committing himself to its proper execution nor decisively terminating it in light of his wife's unhappiness. His attention moves back and forth between doing Peduzzi's bidding and attempting to mollify his wife. Assigning her the task of carrying the fishing rods that she has no interest in using and that are clear reminders of his insistence on illegal activity, he proceeds to bully her into keeping up with him and Peduzzi. Finally, she acidly remarks the half-heartedness of his attempted apology in the Concordia, in which he simultaneously chides her for not having worn another sweater and expresses concern over her being cold. Her castigating reply that she is already wearing three sweaters calls attention to his lack of perceptiveness and insensitivity.

While the question of the abortion is settled by the story's end, one suspects that even more fundamental problems lie at the heart of the marriage. In a story that has skillfully shifted the narrative focus from character to character, one point of view — Tiny's — is absent from the ending, for she has returned to the hotel. Peduzzi is satisfied, his dreams of a better station in life amplified by the Marsala he has drunk. The husband's change of heart and subsequent relief are paralleled by the final atmospheric changes. But Tiny knows none of this, and her reply at the Concordia that "None of it makes any difference" hangs over the ending like a storm cloud. "I'm sorry I talked the way I did at lunch," her husband has said to her. "We were both getting at the same thing from different angles" (99). Her depressed reply is disturbing for its sweeping glumness, and it is puzzling in that she does not bother to counter his lame version of their quarrel. Since she is opposed to having an abortion, and he was apparently the one proposing it, it is difficult to see how they were "both getting at the same thing." His obvious illogic reflects a weak and self-serving attempt to mollify her and salvage the day, for at this point in the story he has not yet experienced a change of heart. The fact that she is too weary or too angry to refute this obvious piece of sophistry indicates that he has been wearing away at her for some time and that she believes that attempts at communication are futile. The scene plays like a worn-out record.

"Cross-Country Snow" is the fourth successive piece to treat the theme of marriage and pregnancy. Since this time no wife is actually present in the story, the only point of view examined is that of the husband — in this case, Nick Adams. In two senses the story picks up where things have left off. First, it returns us to Nick's history in chronological and developmental order. He was last seen, in "Chapter VI," having been injured in the war; this story places him on a ski trip in postwar Europe, the effects of his injury evident in the way he skis. "Cross-Country Snow" also continues the progression within the group of four marital stories whose topics have advanced thus: a couple's frustrated but perhaps not deeply felt desire to have a baby ("A Very Short Story"); a wife's strong desire to have a baby frustrated by her husband ("Cat in the Rain"); a husband urging his resistant wife to have an abortion ("Out of Season"); and now a man trying to reconcile himself to the fait accompli of his impending fatherhood. There is no talk of abortion in this story; the subject is fatherhood pulling back on the reins of masculine autonomy.

In the opening scenes Hemingway captures the physical sensations of skiing, the exhilaration and sense of freedom that Nick feels and George apparently shares. But limitation and mutability are key themes of the story — not freedom, which is shown to be contingent rather than absolute. As they make their run down the mountain, George telemarks through the deep snow and expresses his admiration for Nick's Christy turn. But Nick reveals that he has made a virtue of necessity, explaining, "I can't telemark with my leg" (108). He carries his war injury with him and has managed to overcome its effects; but he remains ever mindful of it, for it is there to remind him, like it or not.

Images of self-control in the midst of outdoor physical activity are key and were introduced in "Chapter XII," the vignette that precedes "Cross-Country Snow" and that depicts the bullfighter Villalta in his moment of triumph. Likewise, physical mastery will play a major thematic role in the final Nick story, "Big Two-Hearted

River." In "Cross-Country Snow" Hemingway shows Nick "crouching so he was almost sitting back on his skis, trying to keep the center of gravity low, the snow driving like a sand-storm, he knew the pace was too much. But he held it. He would not let go and spill" (107). That Nick does spill on the first segment of the run does not take away from the significance of this temporary command, especially in light of his injury. The discipline and the effort are what matter, not faultless execution. Nick is beginning to develop an ethic whereby the compensations one receives from an activity are felt in proportion to its inherent difficulty and also, and more important, to the self-mastery and the overcoming of personal obstacles it requires. He has traveled some distance from the young man in "The Three-Day Blow" who was ready to go out and drunkenly bang away with his gun at anything he and Bill might "jump" in the woods.

Yet, Nick's fledgling self-mastery must be placed in the broader context of adult life, where circumstances are sure to arise and then exact their consequences. Nick is troubled by Helen's pregnancy, and in the second half of the story, which takes place in a local tavern, the mood of the men shifts abruptly when George introduces a discussion of Nick's impending fatherhood. The previous conversational fluidity and the relatively expansive mood produced in Nick by the skiing are brought to a halt when George asks whether Helen is pregnant. When Nick answers tersely, George tries to draw him out on the subject but receives a series of monosyllabic replies. Finally, George sees that Nick is not elated with the prospects of fatherhood:

> George sat silent. He looked at the empty bottle and the empty glasses.
> "It's hell, isn't it?" he said. (111)

The empty bottle and the empty glass, of course, serve as metaphors for the brevity of experience, and Nick is grown up enough to realize that one cannot ski forever. The bottom of the last hill comes, and then what? Krebs in "Soldier's Home" believed that he just needed some time to readjust, to find a way to make his life uncomplicated. Nick has apparently resigned himself to the fact that complications necessarily exist, for his answer to George's question, "It's hell, isn't it?", intended as rhetorical, is "No. Not exactly" (111).

The "no" signals Nick's resignation. The "not exactly" bespeaks two things. In part it expresses normal misgivings about beginning any new stage of life, especially one that brings the uncertainties and responsibilities of fatherhood, and in part it indicates Nick's last vestiges of adolescence.

These vestiges are apparent elsewhere in the story: in the youthful feel of the talk and the childlike quality of some of the young men's expressions, in the shared desire to "just bum together" across the Alps, and in Nick's merely tentative adoption of the role of expert or "older man." Nick is, by turns, mature enough to be sensitive to the waitress's possible predicament but immature in dismissing that sympathetic perception with the flippant comment that "no girls get married around here till they're knocked up" (110). The second half of the story turns on being "knocked up," for Helen is pregnant and Nick plans to assume the duties of fatherhood. It is also possible that she and Nick are not married. The story does not mention marriage; and the waitress's being "knocked up" and single could very well parallel his and Helen's situation: for Nick is perceptive about the waitress's condition but also seems to need to dismiss it.

Although "Cross-Country Snow" is not as fully realized as the best stories in the volume, it would be a mistake to dismiss it too lightly, for in it Nick shows signs of learning a crucial lesson. He takes a decisive step in his maturation, realizing that pleasures are provisional and that there is no hiding from that fact. Nick is prepared to see things through with Helen, and he does know that boyhood ends. Yet, one does not cease attending to the good things in life because they are provisional; rather, knowing that they are so makes their pursuit all the more necessary and all the more valuable. To George's question about skiing after his return to the United States, Nick answers that the mountains are "too rocky. There's too much timber and they're too far away" (111). And while he declares that the freedom represented by skiing makes life worthwhile, he is also mature enough to recognize that "there isn't any good in promising" to do it at a later time. At the end of "The Three-Day Blow" Nick still believed that you could go back to things. At the end of "Cross-Country Snow" he realizes that you may not even be able to go on to new things. Circumstances may serve to restrict;

there are always consequences. Yet, in the story's final stage Nick re-affirms a commitment in the face of contingency. He may not be able to ski forever, not even for much longer, but he is skiing now, and that is the fact of the moment that matters. Do not waste experience. Do not waste opportunity. Thus the final sentence, narrated by the omniscient narrator but seemingly shared by Nick's consciousness: "Now they would have the run home together" (112). This final optimistic turn in the story is noteworthy in a volume that heretofore has favored the flat ending, or the last paragraph as dying fall or ironic twist. Such optimism signals growth in Nick; but a great trial awaits him in the volume's final story.[17]

"My Old Man": A One-Story Interlude

"My Old Man" temporarily puts the reader on hold with Nick. Of all the stories in the book, its placement is the most problematic: it focuses on a boy, but the volume's generic protagonist has already progressed into the first years of adulthood. A partial answer to the placement problem — and it is one that we can be sure that Hemingway considered, even if we are not satisfied with his decision[18] —

---

[17] Nancy R. Comley and Robert Scholes, apparently setting aside the optimistic tone generated at the story's end, have given an interesting and ultimately darker reading of the story than the one I am offering here. Aligning this story with elements of "Indian Camp," they write: "In many of these early tales it seems as if what is being resisted is merely paternity itself and its attendant responsibilities, but there is also evidence in the larger Hemingway Text indicating that to father a son is to write your own death warrant" (15). While their reading is deeply informed, it seems troublesome to their interpretation that in "Cross-Country Snow" neither Nick nor the reader yet knows whether or not Nick's child is going to be a son, though a subsequently published story, "Fathers and Sons," makes clear that Nick does have at least one boy.

[18] Paul Smith writes that in a preliminary arrangement of the volume Hemingway "considered switching the places of 'The Three-Day Blow" and 'My Old Man.'" (118, JFK Collection item 97A). This would seem an odd place to consider inserting the story as opposed to one story earlier, for the boy in "My Old Man" is clearly a preteen, while Nick is in his late teens in "The End of Something," which would have preceded it if

lies not in the narrative focus but in the narrative voice, which is that of the boy, now grown into a man, looking back on the disillusioning experience of his father's death. Yet this answer is only partly satisfactory, because, although it is clear that the narrator is telling his story from a mature perspective, he occasionally adopts the "Gee" and "Say" mannerisms of his boyhood. The time referred to by the "now" in the first sentence is never made exact: "I guess looking at it, now, my old man was cut out for a fat guy . . ." (115). Based on the story's placement in the volume and on the sort of retrospective judgment the story implies, "now" should be taken to refer to the narrator speaking as a young adult.

The story begins with Joe Butler remembering the period his father spent as a jockey in Italy. Staying in shape is not easy for Joe's dad, but he has the self-discipline to work out daily to keep his weight down. His keeping in professional trim and his work with the horses are set at odds with a less distinguished facet of his character: in the past he has helped to fix races. At some point, however, he decided to change his ways, so when he wins the Premio Commercio, it is not a moment of clear and clean triumph for him because he had apparently been instructed not to win. This double-crossing of the race fixers leads to the father and son leaving Italy for Paris. Still, it is not correct to see Joe's father as a now-honest man struggling in a corrupt sport — not yet. He has cheated in the past; he had agreed to cheat at the Premio Commercio but changed his mind, and this decision may have been an attempt to turn over a new leaf but equally may have been odds-tampering or double-dealing to his own advantage — cheating within cheating. In Paris the elder Butler will buy his own horse and attempt to win on the up and up, but not before betting on inside tips on fixed races. One such race is described in detail. A magnificent horse named Kzar could have walked away with the race but is purposely held back to place. "It sure took a great jock to keep that Kzar horse from win-

---

this provisional order had been adopted. Placing the story before "The End of Something" would have solved this problem of chronology as well as avoided splitting up "The End of Something" and its companion piece, "The Three-Day Blow."

ning," Joe's father says. Joe describes this race as a moral turning point for himself, but just why this is so is not precisely clear:

> Of course I knew it was funny [a fixed race] all the time. But my old man saying that right out like that sure took the kick all out of it for me and I didn't get the real kick back ever again . . . . (124)

The moral crisis is dependent on Joe's admiration for Kzar and comes to a head when his father actually utters the words about cheating. That the horse's nobility is cheapened is easy to understand, but it is unclear why Joe's father's words wound him more deeply than his active participation in the plot to prevent the horse from winning. In the end Joe's father puts together a stake and wins a horse, Gilford, which he rides in a race in which he intends to compete honestly. He is doing well in the race when he is killed in a fall. As Joe is being escorted from the track by George Gardner, he overhears two men disparaging his father for the cheating in which the latter had engaged in the past. In the last lines of the story Joe thinks, "But I don't know. Seems like when they get started they don't leave a guy with nothing" (129). First the father had helped to betray Kzar; now, attempting to ride cleanly and do his honest best, he has fallen victim to circumstances. Ironically, George Gardner had been the jockey who rode Kzar in the fixed race, and from his untrustworthy lips come the words intended for comfort: "don't listen to what those bums said, Joe. Your old man was one swell guy" (129).

While I would argue that *In Our Time* might be a stronger volume without "My Old Man," the story does maintain topical and thematic consistency with the stories that immediately precede it. All of them, beginning with "The Revolutionist," treat the disillusionment of expatriates adrift in the modern world. The story also recalls "Indian Camp" and "The Doctor and the Doctor's Wife" in its depiction of the imperfect father brought to bay by his weaknesses. In this respect it is closer to "Indian Camp," since in both stories the father is brought low in the act of doing good. The story also continues the theme that has followed Nick since "The Three-Day Blow," the impossibility of going back. In "Cross-Country Snow"

Nick knows enough not to make any promises about "going back" to skiing. He has learned that it may not always be possible to return to that which you have loved. Joe's father tries to return to clean racing after fixing races, only to be thrown from his horse and killed. There is no cause-and-effect relationship between his past dishonesty and the accident, for contrived "poetic justice" is not part of Hemingway's stock in trade. To the young Joe his father's death must have seemed capricious. The older, narrating Joe may realize, along with the reader, that once one has sold out something that is dear, once one has betrayed his craft, he may not get a second chance. In a world where winners and losers alike may take nothing, where each person must struggle to develop his own moral center, that center, once obtained, should not be put at risk. This theme will be worked out with great poignancy in *The Sun Also Rises* in the contrastive relationship between Jake Barnes and Pedro Romero.

"My Old Man," more directly than any other story in the volume, shows the influence of Sherwood Anderson, who had already published his famous "I Want to Know Why," which also treats a boy who loves horse racing and culminates in the boy's disillusionment with a man. But one can also see why Hemingway began to bridle when critics compared him to Anderson, however well intended the comparisons may have been. Despite the Andersonesque qualities of "My Old Man," it is clear that even this early in his career Hemingway had begun to outdistance his mentor. Picking up on Anderson's use of the vernacular, Hemingway achieves a more informal, more fluid voice. He more fully effaces what Pound meant by the "licherary." Anderson's stories often retain a flavor, however faint, of the nineteenth century, and he can be prone to a sort of sentimentalism that Hemingway's taut style and more uncompromising irony all but eliminate from the latter's earliest work. Even though the story is narrated in the first person, it retains the show-don't-tell methodology typical of the volume. Joe does not explain his feelings, either at the time of his father's death or "now," but leaves them for the reader to infer. This task is made ambiguous by the fact that Joe seems alternately innocent and wise in the story, at once unable to explain exactly what went on in Italy but able to say that he knew about his father getting in on the fixed Kzar race. What we do know is that one disreputable adult receives the compliments of another at the end of the story, and that this is cold comfort to Joe.

"Big Two-Hearted River": An American Masterpiece

Hemingway labored long and hard at "Big Two-Hearted River," knowing that it would be the crown of his first full-length, commercially published volume. As he worked, he must have had James Joyce's tour de force "The Dead" in mind, for that long story ended *Dubliners* with the sort of signature piece that Hemingway hoped to create. Composed over a six-month period, "Big Two-Hearted River" ends the volume as it began, with Nick Adams in the woods of northern Michigan — only this time grown up, tested by life, and subjected to the trials of his time. When the book was published, Hemingway, in a letter to F. Scott Fitzgerald, graded "Big Two-Hearted River" and "Indian Camp" as the stories with which he was most satisfied (24/12/1925: *SL* 180). The long struggle to write the story seemed worth it. He had brought the volume full circle.

On first reading "Big Two-Hearted River," Fitzgerald had told Hemingway that the piece could not sustain the interest of readers, because Hemingway "had written a story in which nothing happened" (Baker, *The Writer* 125). Fitzgerald undoubtedly came around to seeing what his fellow writer was doing sooner than most, and the story did gain early appreciation; but it took some time for readers to develop an awareness of the story's depths. This lag in critical appreciation testifies to Hemingway's subtlety and to the adage that new art must develop its own audience. To this day inexperienced readers may characterize the story as an accomplished account of a solitary fishing trip, detailed but devoid of drama. The descriptions of fishing and camping are vivid and meticulous — Hemingway had taught himself to fulfill Joseph Conrad's famous charge to the writer, "by the power of the written word, to make you [the reader] hear, to make you feel . . . to make you *see*" — but the reader familiar with Hemingway's method knows that the true drama lies beneath the surface of the story.

As Part One of the story begins, Nick watches a train disappear through the burned-over landscape of Upper Michigan. He has been dropped off in Seney to begin a solitary trout-fishing and camping trip. The place is a ghost town, having recently been swept over by the fire that has blackened the landscape. From the railroad bridge Nick watches the fish in the river, and "his heart tightened as the trout moved. He felt all the old feeling," anticipating the excitement of fishing such as he had done with his buddies in the past (134). Nick has a heavy pack to carry, and the day is hot, but he is happy as he hikes, observing the terrain and noticing the grasshoppers, which are blackened "from living in the burned-over land" (136). Nick plans his route so as to postpone his arrival at the river until he has exacted a full day's walk from himself. After a nap, Nick awakes just in time to make it to the river before sunset. As Part One comes to an end, Nick sets up his simple camp, taking care to do everything properly so that he creates "the good place." He prepares a modest meal of canned food and reminisces about his old fishing companion Hopkins while he makes coffee, but his memories are becoming too much for him to handle, so he "chokes" them down and falls asleep in his tent.

Part Two begins the following morning with Nick catching grasshoppers for bait. He is excited and eager to begin fishing, but first he makes a breakfast of buckwheat cakes and apple butter. Pleased with his camp, he packs a simple lunch and readies himself for fishing. He fishes with pleasure and expertise, taking care to do everything properly. His mindfulness sets him apart from the careless fishermen who "spoil it" for those who truly love the activity. As with his making of the camp the previous night, the routine verges on ritual as he catches three fish and cleans two of them. He consciously works to maintain the pleasure of the day. He must go slowly: he cannot handle too much excitement. He feels that he is not ready to fish the nearby swamp, for there "the fishing would be tragic" (155). Staying within the bounds of what he can handle, pleased with the day, maintaining his careful and orderly adventure, Nick heads back to his "good" camp, holding off the swamp for the days ahead.

Careful is the word that applies to Nick's activities not only in the sense of caution and control but also in the sense of demonstrating proper concern for that which is worthy: full of care. Nick is neither carefree nor careless. He is careful to the point of meticulousness. This is a story where over two pages are devoted to describing the simplest supper imaginable. The reader must wait with Nick for half a paragraph while his canned beans and spaghetti cool down enough to eat. Two-thirds of a page are devoted to the pitching of his tent. This is surely what Fitzgerald meant when he said that nothing happens in the story. But to put it that way is to overlook two important factors: the skill with which Hemmingway describes nature and Nick's activities in it, and the true source of drama in the story — Nick's mind, which, more than anything else, must be treated with care. His outdoorsman's skill, his patience, his proficiency in trout fishing, his solicitude for the proper way of doing things, his planning of a simple routine — all these qualities are conspicuous in his activities, and they link his past to his present in a useful way not often found in the stories. These are the skills to which young Nick had been exposed in boyhood and that he clearly came to love as a teenager.[19] Now they are put to service in a sort of self-therapy. All is not well with Nick, and he is out in the woods to recuperate.

The purposefulness of Nick's relaxation is evident, but the reasons for it are only hinted at. In "The Battler" (which likewise begins on train tracks in the Michigan countryside) Ad showed that life can "get you in the head" and make you "not quite right," and Bugs seemed to promise Nick that the time would come when he, too, would have to battle for control of his own mind. Thus it is that in Nick's thoughts of Hopkins we see the first clear indication that he is struggling to maintain control over himself: "His mind was starting to work. He knew he could choke it because he was tired enough" (142). These sentences explain why Nick wants to tire himself out with a full day's walk before settling down to camp: fatigue is his ally in achieving psychic ease. Besides tiring himself out, keeping himself busy is apparently necessary, but only within the bounds of what he can handle. While the precariousness of Nick's mind is not immedi-

---

[19] In a long section deleted from the published version of the story, Hemingway wrote that Nick had been "married to" fishing. "Really married to it. It wasn't any joke." The section is published as "On Writing" in *The Nick Adams Stories* (234).

ately evident, early on it is clear that he is making a vacation trip in the literal sense of the word *vacation:* an emptying out. Hot and tired as he walks through the fire-scarred country, "Nick felt happy. He felt he had left everything behind, the need for thinking, the need to write, other needs. It was all back of him" (134). Here again is the emphasis on physical activity purchasing peace of mind, but exactly what besides thinking and writing is included in the "everything" that must be "left behind" is not made clear here or anywhere in the story. Readers must decide for themselves.

Nick has by now suffered his share of the pain and loss and disillusionment that constitute the volume's emotional core. In "Cross-Country Snow" he was anxious about his impending fatherhood and the attendant responsibilities, which will necessarily hamper his freedom. It is probable, then, that in order to support Helen, Nick returned from Europe without feeling ready to do so. He may also have come back to marry her, if, as seemed to be suggested in "Cross-Country Snow," the pregnancy occurred out of wedlock.[20] Such anxieties could well be a part of the "everything" that he needs to leave behind, but those sorts of growing pains, by themselves, would seem insufficient to produce the fragility of mind apparent when Nick loses the first big trout he hooks: "Nick's hand was shaky. He reeled in slowly. The thrill had been too much. He felt, vaguely, a little sick, as though it would be better to sit down" (150). From other stories we know that Nick is extremely sensitive, but here he is truly fighting for self-control. Perhaps it is the accumulation of life's knocks that has produced such mental fragility. Perhaps, also, one telling incident has affected Nick more than any other, has left him nearly broken. If so, that incident could be his wounding in the war — the war that was the pivotal event in Nick's

---

[20] The themes of marriage and fishing are interwoven more overtly and at some length in "On Writing." There Hemingway shows Nick to be pondering the idea that he had "admitted by marrying [Helen] that something was more important than fishing." He then thinks of conventional marriage as "this fake ideal planted in you and then you lived your life to it," concluding that "all the love went into fishing and the summer" (234–235).

life and the pivotal event for his generation. In *A Farewell to Arms* Frederic Henry will desert, leaving behind the world of rhetoric turned absurd in favor of erotic love and the concrete pleasures of the day. While the enticements of erotic love play no such role in Nick's decision, he, like Frederic Henry, makes his own separate peace in "Chapter VI." Not a patriot after his wounding, he, too, realizes that the daily pleasures of the physical are the only thing that matter and, indeed, are his only hope for inner rehabilitation. But making a separate peace may be more easily said than done.

The war is present in more than Nick's subjectivity. As he did in "The End of Something," Hemingway begins "Big Two-Hearted River" with a descriptive paragraph that serves as an objective correlative for the story's emotional landscape. Just as Hemingway had prepared the reader for the breakup of Nick and Marjorie in his description of the ghost town Hortons Bay, at the outset of "Big Two-Hearted River" he focuses on the burned-over landscape through which Nick walks in search of a better place. The imagery, right down to the blackened grasshoppers he scrutinizes, parallels Nick's burned-out state of mind. Hemingway again participates in the literary buildup of wasteland imagery found in other groundbreaking postwar literature. The northern Michigan countryside of "Big Two-Hearted River" invokes the cultural memory of the devastated landscapes of the First World War. Nick cannot help but drag the painful remnants of the war with him to the wilds of the Upper Peninsula, where he will endeavor to teach himself how to hold them at bay through ritualized outdoor experience that recalls his more carefree youth.

The country here is more than mere landscape for Nick: it is the fundamental element through which he will assert his effort to soothe himself. But landscape was important to Hemingway in its own right. He cared mightily about making his nature painting come alive, a desire evident in a letter he wrote to Gertrude Stein after finishing "Big Two-Hearted River": "Nothing happens and the country is swell. I'm trying to do the country like Cezanne [*sic*] and having a hell of a time and sometimes getting it a little bit"

(15/8/1924: *SL* 122).[21] Hemingway did, indeed, achieve in words something of the master's never-hasty painterly effects, which emphasized formal construction. Scenes are rendered by blocking out the fundamental constituents of form and color, yet they retain the sense of a harmonious whole. Like Cézanne, Hemingway was in love with the very geography of certain areas, and he often rendered his landscapes by giving primary attention to the way color planes structure the countryside. Flooding the scene with sun and heat, Hemingway writes of Nick's hike:

> The road ran on, dipping occasionally, but always climbing. Nick went on up. Finally the road after going parallel to the burnt hillside reached the top. Nick leaned back against a stump and slipped out of the pack harness. Ahead of him, as far as he could see, was the pine plain. The burned country stopped off at the left with the range of hills. On ahead islands of dark pine trees rose out of the plain. Far off to the left was the line of the river. Nick followed it with his eye and caught glints of the water in the sun. (135)

Thomas Hermann has pointed out that only selectively does Hemingway give over a paragraph solely to description; description is almost always combined with the reporting of action (33). Scenes are painted through the heart's eye. In the deleted ending to the story Hemingway had written of Cézanne from Nick's point of view: "He [Nick] wanted to write like Cezanne [*sic*] painted. . . . Nobody had ever written about country like that. He felt almost holy about it. It was deadly serious. You could do it if you would fight it out. If you'd lived right with your eyes. . . . He was going to work on it until he got it" (*Nick Adams Stories* 239).

---

[21] It was Stein who urged Hemingway to drop his original ending of the story with the famous statement that "remarks are not literature." The remarks she had in mind were the eight pages of interior monologue now titled "On Writing," wherein Nick reminisces about fishing, ponders the importance of marriage, and considers contemporary writers such as James Joyce. Hemingway was wise in this instance to follow Stein's advice. While extremely interesting for the student of Hemingway, the ending would have made the story much more diffuse.

Unlike many Hemingway stories, "Big Two-Hearted River" shows that it may be possible to go back, but only if one does so under the right conditions: alone, with discipline and purpose and with limited expectations. Nick feels "all the old feeling" when he first looks down into the two-hearted river, but this trip is different from those of his adolescence because Nick is different. The swamp is not something to be plunged into with the careless bravado of inexperienced youth but something to be saved until one has the inner reserves required for its challenge. Nick knows all about fishing in the swamp, which implies that he has done it before, but now he would be fishing it more fully aware of its complications and potential consequences. In the external terrain of the fishing story the swamp requires expertise and daring and the willingness to face disappointment and loss. Things can become too unpredictable there. In regard to Nick's inner terrain the swamp suggests his continued fear, his continued fragility, and, on a more hopeful note, his self-awareness. It is a sign of his maturity that he does not bull ahead but decides to stay within himself.

Thus, the precision Nick devotes to simple activities is remarkable in itself, but it is also a key element in his recuperation. In its most literal, narrow sense, of course, to *recuperate* means to get something back. Nick lives in the same rootless and alienating world as the Revolutionist and Krebs. With them he shares wartime and expatriate experiences, and like them he is nervously exhausted and preoccupied. Unlike them, however, Nick is in the process of creating his own structures for living. The precise circumstances of Nick's life outside this camping trip are not explicitly given, but something of those circumstances can be inferred from his attitude to the tent that he so painstakingly pitches. In actuality the most temporary sort of shelter, for Nick it becomes the best place he has found on this successful day. For many a camper a tent is something to endure, part of the price one pays for an extended outing in nature, but for Nick the tent becomes a substitute home, quite possibly the first home he has found for some time:

> Already there was something mysterious and homelike. Nick was happy as he crawled inside the tent. He had not been unhappy all day. This was different though. Now things were done. There

had been this to do. Now it was done. It had been a hard trip. He was very tired. That was done. He had made his camp. He was settled. Nothing could touch him. It was a good place to camp. He was there, in the good place. He was in his home where he had made it. (139)

Here style is in absolute service to content, the short declarative sentences echoing both Nick's methodical construction of the camp and his continued need for simplicity and controlled action. By keeping things simple, the repetitions drive home Nick's self-created domestic ease. The repetition of forms of the verb *to do* emphasizes the story's work-as-play-as-therapy motif. The prominence of *home* and *good* together reinforces the theme of Nick's previous restlessness and his need to return to fundamental principles. The subtle use of the double negative "He had *not* been *un*happy all day" reinforces the bad state of things for Nick before the trip, positing a neutral state ("not unhappy") as something positive. Tired but settled, Nick makes himself content by creating a deliberately simplified retreat into his new womblike home. From this cocoon, perhaps a metamorphosed Nick will eventually emerge.

Images of retreat into the woods have reoccurred in the volume, but in Nick's previous adventures retreating has not signaled a positive advance. In "The Battler" retreat indicates at best a tentativeness on Nick's part, in "The Three-Day Blow" self-deception, and in "The Doctor and the Doctor's Wife" the immaturity of childhood. Each of these stories ended with Nick walking off into the woods after a troubling episode but did not convey the sense that he had digested his rich experiences to any perceptible degree. Certainly none shows him capable of dealing with his experiences. While "Big Two-Hearted River" remains tentative in that Nick is clearly not completely healed by one day's fishing (after all, how could he be?), it does end more affirmatively. The story shows that retreat is not a sign of immaturity or passivity when it is undertaken with a conscious design. Likewise with nature, which has consistently been shown as a soothing force in the stories, but heretofore only accidentally so. In "Big Two-Hearted River" Nick enters nature with an adult consciousness and purposefulness. Nick trailing his hand in the water at the end of "Indian Camp" is simply too young to comprehend his mortality. Nick fishing selected spots on the river is mature enough to know that it is two-hearted, divided like himself. It is a sign of his maturity that he can recognize his own limitations and that he comes to nature at the end of the book knowing that all things are contingent and fragile — the human heart and mind most of all.

5: The Interchapters and the World of *In Our Time*: "The Picture of the Whole"

CHAPTER THREE OF THIS STUDY DISCUSSED THE IMPACT of the vignettes on the formal status of *In Our Time*, taking into account Hemingway's own statements on the matter. We saw that while these statements are illuminating and suggestive, they do not tell the complete story of either the creative origins or the aesthetic effects of the interchapters. Whatever his intentions for the volume, and whenever these intentions began to be realized, Hemingway certainly had to be aware that alternating two different kinds of fiction in a book containing thirty-two separate compositions would create a formal complexity not found even in such modern predecessors as Joyce. While it would be impossible to discuss the hundreds of permutations and combinations made possible by thirty-two fictions in relation to one another, this chapter will examine some of the vignettes' salient features, emphasizing significant connections that they make one with another.

Broadly speaking, the vignettes treat three subjects: eight are about war, including two that can more properly be said to be about the immediate aftereffects of war — execution and house arrest; six are about bullfighting; and two deal with criminals. Clearly, the vignettes are preoccupied with violence, and even with the passage of seven modern decades to jade us, they still have the power to shock. But shock value alone cannot explain their continuing hold on readers, nor the variety and complexity of the responses that they generate. These effects can only be accounted for by levels of meaning that transcend the merely sensational.

The new century had already proven itself inescapably dangerous and exceedingly violent, and, while Hemingway's insistence on the violent was surely a matter of temperament and experience, it was much more importantly a declaration that the writers of his generation had better face up to the fact that the established, stable values that had held off certain kinds of violence were no longer functional. A thorough accounting of "our time" would have to include a diligent study of violence. It is worth noting the degree to which the various acts of violence depicted in the vignettes blur the lines between socially approved brutality and that which is considered illegal or immoral. This blurring is pushed to such a troubling extent that several of the vignettes take on an absurdist tinge. Conversely, the cruelty and blood of the bullring, while often imperfect in execution, derive from an attempt to impose order on violence. Finally, the sensational nature of the vignettes provides a crucible for Hemingway's style. The appalling events depicted would seem most naturally to lend themselves to verbal excess, and in the hands of a lesser writer could well have prompted overwrought language. But Hemingway's instincts led him in the opposite direction: toward the cool portrayal, the tight linguistic control, and the understated irony that comprise the vignettes' dominant register.

The absurdist tinge is evident in several war vignettes, the first of which recounts a drunken march during the First World War. In "Chapter I" the lieutenant heading up the unit is hardly the ideal of chivalry and order who commands respect from his troops. He farcically races his horse to and fro, announcing to it and to the world the patently obvious fact that he is roaring drunk. Just as farcically, the adjutant insists that the narrator put out his kitchen fire for fear that the enemy will observe it, even though they are still fifty kilometers from the front. It is implied that the narrator has been able to develop his absurdist stance because he is telling the story from a distanced, mature, knowing point of view. The story ends with his statement "That was when I was a kitchen corporal," suggesting that with more war experience under his belt he would now take such absurdities as a matter of course. What today's reader may not realize is the price at which the narrator's knowledge and maturity were bought. E. R. Hagemann has pointed out that the Champagne offensive to which the soldiers are headed resulted in 120,000 French casualties in its first three weeks and 145,000 in three months (53). Sardonically humorous as this vignette is on its own, in the light of the succeeding war vignettes it appears even more absurd: their cumulative effect is to reveal that while modern warfare has deprived people of traditional notions of dignity and honor, it has provided nothing in their stead.

The First World War quickly proved to millions that any residual ideals of martial grace and chivalry that they still held would have to be jettisoned. There is little nobility to be seen in the war vignettes, which depict cruel or senseless acts. Their anonymous narrators seem wounded in their souls from the accumulated effects of modern warfare. "Chapter II," for instance, depicts the flight of Greek Christians from Thrace that Hemingway had witnessed during his coverage of the Greco-Turkish war. Here the Greek cavalry "herds along" the refugees in a rain-soaked scene of misery and chaos. The soldiers have been given the militarily ignoble task of supervising a retreat that, presumably, their army's failure on the battlefield has necessitated. "Chapter III" and "Chapter IV" show that killing in wartime looks very much like murder. In each case the enemy is pot shot as they climb over a wall.

"Chapter III" replicates in miniature the Great War's many senseless frontal assaults, wherein men scrambled up out of the trenches only to be mowed down in an utterly mechanical fashion. The speaker here, as in the succeeding vignette, is apparently a for- mer British officer: "We waited till he got one leg over and then potted him. . . . Then three more came over further down the wall. We shot them. They all came just like that" (29). While it is possible to argue that the narrators in this vignette and the next express sat- isfaction with remembered instances of easy success in killing the en- emy (interpreted along these lines, "Chapter IV" reveals an outright bloodthirstiness), I see these pieces as embodying the voices of will- fully hard-shelled men engaged in oblique expressions of remorse. The verb *potted*, emphasizing the unheroic, unchivalrous nature of killing in modern war, is used in "Chapter III" and again in "Chap- ter IV," both of whose narrators speak with the same detached, slightly embittered sort of voice heard in "On the Quai at Smyrna."[1]

---

[1] Literally, of course, these narrators can be viewed as personae quite simi- lar to, but actually distinct from, one another. It may be that three sepa- rate characters, or two, or one, are present in these three fictions, but the

The British flavor and the repetitions ("frightfully," "priceless," "topping," "put out") carry an ironic force that echoes each narrator's disgust with the debased business of plugging men from a safe distance. And, as happens in each of the first four chapters, the narrator tells his story in the knowing tones of ironic self-protection, his callousness disguising the soul-wounding he has undergone. While the war was undoubtedly disillusioning for all who saw frontline combat, for a certain sort of romantic soul and for an earnest sort of gentleman officer the loss of noble military conceptions must have been deeply troubling. For such men an integral component of their worldview, an aspect of their very sense of identity was shattered.

"Chapter V" links up thematically and tonally with the other war vignettes, but particularly, as Hemingway himself noted, refers to "Chapter II" and anticipates "L'Envoi," the volume's concluding piece: "The refugees leave Thrace, due to the Greek ministers, who are shot. The whole thing closes with the talk with the King of Greece and his Queen in their Garden" (*SL* 91–92). A detailed examination of this vignette will serve to exemplify both the literary quality typical of these short pieces and the resonance they achieve in relation to one another. While Hemingway was familiar with the issues of the Greco-Turkish war and had arrived late on the scene to cover the disastrous Greek retreat through Thrace, he did not report on the execution of the cabinet ministers who were held responsible for the fiasco by the new Greek regime. It is one of the noteworthy instances in the book where a writer commonly thought to offer barely fictionalized transcriptions of direct experience depicts an event he has not actually witnessed.

There is no dirtier, grimmer, more dismal vignette than this one, which is painted with an ironic eye worthy of Goya. With its shutters all "nailed shut," the hospital has ceased to be a place of healing and has become a place of retribution — a jail and a gallows. The scene is absolutely impersonal, beginning with the first word: "They" shoot the hapless, nameless ministers, just as "they" will hang Sam Cardinella early in the morning in "Chapter XV." In that vignette, de-

---

more telling fact would seem to be the overlapping features they display when they speak.

spite the priests' exhortations for him to "be a man," Sam Cardinella will not be able to stand and will defecate in his pants, leading the guards who have been holding him up first to drop him and then to sit him on a chair. That scene has its precise antecedent here in the minister who is ill from typhoid. Unable to stand or to be propped up by his guards, he is left to meet his death sitting down in a puddle of dirty water, slumped over ignobly "with his head on his knees" (52). He is placed, along with the other five ministers, against a wall that is, like the many walls in other vignettes, a locus of death. In his short declarative sentences Hemingway repeats the simple key words *wall* and, as in the following passage, *water* and *rain*, creating effects reminiscent of imagist poetry: "There were pools of water in the courtyard. There were wet dead leaves on the paving of the courtyard. It rained hard" (52). Modifiers are almost absent, and the few that are used are there to paint the scene. The leaves are "wet" and "dead." The ministers stand "very quietly," apparent exemplars of stoicism in an otherwise utterly unheroic scene. Nowhere does the narrator tell us how anyone feels but lets the scene, as painted, speak for itself. No film director could have done better. The courtyard, originally constructed to be a place of beauty and a center of social interaction, has become the grim, isolated locale where death is summarily meted out. (In other vignettes gardens are used to similar ironic effect.) The hard rain falling on the scene connects the ministers with "the old men and women, soaked through" by the rain in "Chapter II," victims of the miscalculations for which these ministers are now being scapegoated. Rain and water, ordinarily used in literature as archetypal symbols of renewal, are here, as they will be in *A Farewell to Arms,* symbols of death that will not lead to rebirth. While he professed to dislike Eliot, Hemingway was quite capable of spinning out his own versions of the modern world as wasteland.

As we have seen, "Chapter VI" is a pivotal moment in the development of Nick Adams. It begins with Nick sitting against a wall, shot in the spine, accompanied by his friend Rinaldi, who is lying face down, apparently injured more severely than Nick. Rinaldi makes "a disappointing audience" for Nick, says the narrator in a typically understated last sentence. Nick has been telling Rinaldi that as far as he is concerned, they are out of the war. They have gained a "separate peace" through their injuries, which involve a change of heart as well as physical disablement. Though they have been wounded in action, and though the battle was "getting forward in the town," and things were "going well" for the Italian army that day, Nick says that he and Rinaldi are "not patriots" any longer (63). Readers of *A Farewell to Arms* will recognize the germ of that novel in this vignette, which also resonates strongly with the immediately subsequent stories and the next interchapter of *In Our Time,* all of which treat wartime disillusionment and heart-hardening.

"Chapter VII" depicts a soldier in an instant of sheer battle terror, promising God a lifetime of dedication in an utterly true-to-life panic-induced torrent of words. But the promises to God are forgotten as quickly as they were made. The young man does not mention Jesus in the brothel he visits the next night, "and he never told anybody" of his promises to God (67). This satirical take on human frailty immediately succeeds "A Very Short Story," another fiction that is heavily dependent on its final sentences for an ironic twist and another in which a young ex-soldier also follows an emotional debacle with an incident of casual sex. The soldier's frightened prayer also anticipates "Soldier's Home," the following story, in which prayer has become equally meaningless for Krebs, for whom, also, carefree liaisons with girls (who are also very likely prostitutes) are apparently more satisfactory than an exacting relationship with God. Girls may give you a dose of the clap, but then again, they may not; and if they do, that can, with luck, be gotten over. The deeper pains of loss and terror and diminishment meted out by war will not be so easy to dismiss. The young men in the war fictions seek the pleasures of the day in a world where the old connections — country, God, home, faithful lady love — have been severed.

After seven consecutive war vignettes, Hemingway withholds his eighth and final one until the end of the volume, significantly titling it "L'Envoi," which in poetic terminology signifies a short and pithy last stanza summarizing a relatively long poem. This final war vignette, like the one describing the ministers' execution, is not a depiction of battle but of war's aftermath. Hemingway finishes here the snapshot chronicle of the Greco-Turkish War that he began in

"On the Quai at Smyrna" and continued in "Chapter II" and "Chapter V." Nicholas Plastiras led a bloodless revolution in 1922, deposing King Constantine, who was succeeded by King George II, who is seen here "working in the garden" (157). It was also Plastiras who had summoned the court martial of the ministers who were executed in "Chapter V."[2] The need for kings has apparently gone the way of God "in our time," for this king is powerless, living under virtual house arrest, a figurehead whose primary goal "is not to be shot [him]self" (157). The antithesis of regal splendor, the king does his own gardening, indulges in the casually cynical statement that the maintenance of power requires that a few heads must roll, and, "like all Greeks," wishes to immigrate to America, promised land of the great unwashed masses. Perhaps the king is unaware of the violent ends to which some of America's immigrant sons come — men such as Sam Cardinella and the Hungarian "wops" found in previous vignettes.

With its tone of jolly cynicism, this final vignette would seem to undercut the provisional hopefulness suggested by "Big Two-Hearted River." Seen in relation to the other vignettes, "L'Envoi" summarizes the nature of the modern world, which can no longer believe in traditional forms of greatness. The Great War was not great. Great men are no longer great (if, indeed, they ever were). Greatness will have to be deliberately achieved in the postwar world of Hemingway's fictions, and it will be measured by a new set of standards that have their source in private, self-generated judgments rather than in the conventional, public realm. Greatness, or its modern substitute, merit, will come not as a birthright but as the product of the sort of self-testing and self-knowledge that Nick begins to demonstrate in "Big Two-Hearted River."

This sort of self-fulfillment by trial can be seen in "Chapter XII," one of six successive bullfight vignettes and the only one in which the torero succeeds unequivocally. A year after the publication of *In Our Time* bullfighting would acquire great importance in *The Sun Also Rises*, in which young Pedro Romero occupies the moral center.

---

[2] Jeffrey Meyers's account of the Greco-Turkish war is especially helpful in clarifying historical background (97–107).

His finesse, his faithfulness to craft, his nobility, and his sexual vitality are forecast in "Chapter XII" in the brief depiction of Villalta in the latter's moment of triumph: "He swung back firmly like an oak when the wind hits it, his legs tight together, the muleta trailing and the sword following the curve behind. . . . Villalta became one with the bull and then it was over. Villalta standing straight and the red hilt of the sword sticking out dully between the bull's shoulders" (105). Hemingway would witness many more bullfights after those he saw prior to writing most of these vignettes (he wrote "Chapter IX" before he had seen even one!). He would refine his feelings and increase his knowledge of tauromachy to such an extent that he would produce a full-length book on the subject, *Death in the Afternoon*. Mistakenly viewed as a sport by many Americans, bullfighting is not an athletic contest, Hemingway realized, but a ritualized confrontation with death. Bullfighting provided one of the few opportunities left for modern man to face danger and death in a deliberate and meaningful way. Hemingway came to see it as part art and part moral testing ground, an occasion contrived for the enactment of the stoical virtues he valued. Most specifically, he came to view it as an embodiment of qualities that he prized in the art of writing, for, as Jeffrey Meyers has said, it "emphasized strict rules, extreme compression, skillful technique . . . and high courage. . . . He thought the writer, like the matador, must create and live his own style; that this style, expressed in art and action, *was* the man" (118). But while he was composing these vignettes, Hemingway's thoughts on the subject were not yet fully developed, for, with the exception of "Chapter XII," they are written in the same ironical key that dominates his vignettes on war and crime.

There is a great deal of blood and gore in the other five bullfighting vignettes, where the carnage is not balanced with any sort of compensatory achievement or nobility. Rather, the emphasis is on failure and shortcoming. In "Chapter IX" two matadors are injured so badly that they must retire. The second has received a thorough goring "against the wall," a location that has by now accumulated deadly overtones from its use in other vignettes. These injuries leave the third bullfighter, "the kid," to kill all five remaining bulls. He succeeds, but the afternoon has become a cruel test of sheer endurance rather than the opportunity to practice graceful bravery that ideally it should be. There is no nobility in the triumph, for in his exhaustion the young bullfighter's legs fail him, and he vomits in full view of the public. In "Chapter X" the picador's horse has its bowels pierced by the bull. The picador, who has tumbled from the horse, displays his bravery by remounting and performing his assigned task, but the focus remains on the less than noble: "The horse's entrails hung down in a blue bunch and swung backward and forward. . . . He cantered jerkily. . . . He stopped stiff. . . . He was nervously wobbly" (89). Hemingway saw the horses, which still fought unprotected by padding in the 1920s, as the comic element of the corrida. Likewise, here, the bull's indecision proves him to be less than a champion. Hesitant in the face of such a clear advantage, he "could not make up his mind to charge" (89).

"Chapter XI" depicts an utterly shameful fiasco in which an unskilled and apparently cowardly bullfighter cannot complete what he has started. By making a pincushion of the bull with "so much bad sticking," he converts the dignified, essentially tragic rhythm of the bullfight into bad comedy (95). This vignette also ends in exhaustion, this time of the bull, who "folded his knees and lay down" and must finally be killed by one of the torero's underlings. The crowd is so incensed that spectators leap the *barrera* (a wall, once again) to punish the torero with the symbolic humiliation of cutting off his pigtail, a form of public emasculation that he has brought on himself. At the end of the vignette the narrator sees him "quite drunk" in a bar, proclaiming that he has suffered such humiliations before because "I am not really a good bullfighter" (95).

"Chapter XIII" begins as "Chapter XI" ends, with a drunken and unprofessional bullfighter making a public spectacle of himself. At the end of "Chapter XI" the narrator sees the bad torero trying to drown his shame in drink, while "Chapter XIII" shows the narrator, who in this instance is himself a bullfighter, trying to get his colleague Luis to come back to the hotel, sober up, and properly prepare for a bullfight. But Luis cannot govern himself, much to the disgust of both the narrator and the day's third bullfighter, Maera, who will have to take on an extra bull because Luis is in no condition to fight. It is Maera who apparently suffers the consequences of

Luis's self-indulgence, for in the subsequent vignette, "Chapter XIV," he is killed by a bull; if "Chapter XIV" is taken to narrate the same day's fights as "Chapter XIII," then it is possible that Maera dies while fighting what should have been Luis's bull. Taken together, these vignettes imply that there are those who debase their calling, while others are there to assume responsibility, and that the world of bullfighting, like the world at large, is equally capable of destroying the good and the bad. Maera's good conduct gains him nothing. He dies while being treated by the same doctor who has been sewing up the wounds of the gashed picador horses. In the world of *In Our Time*, rewards for bravery may not be forthcoming. Both enduring Indian mothers and honorable bullfighters are subject to crude medical attention.

Thus, while "Chapter XII" proves that bullfighting may be a prime field for exemplifying the "grace under pressure" prized by Hemingway, and while it adumbrates the nobility of the good bullfighter that Hemingway would elaborate in future writings, the other vignettes prove that bullfighting is subject to ignobility, defeat, and loss just like any other human endeavor. The death of Maera that ends this sequence points toward the vision of an amoral universe that is later spelled out by Frederic Henry in *A Farewell to Arms*: The world "kills the very good and the very gentle and the very brave impartially" (249). Taken together, the vignettes contribute to the emphasis on disillusionment and loss of ideals that are a hallmark of *In Our Time*.

While part of the vignettes' effectiveness lies in their relationship to one another and part in their juxtaposition to the stories proper, a good deal of their effect is achieved through the highly poetic techniques Hemingway used to render them. It is no wonder that Ezra Pound, the imagist poet, was pleased with the sort of prose Hemingway was honing when he wrote these vignettes, for their essential gesture is to crystallize rather than to narrate. The interchapters do, more or less, tell stories, of course; but they are primarily oriented toward capturing moods and states of mind in a given moment, usually one of crisis. They freeze the moment, objectifying it; and taken as a fragmentarily presented whole, they constitute a cubist picture of the period.

To produce this picture Hemingway uses divers techniques. For one thing, he has created several key images to which he regularly returns. We have already seen the reoccurrence of the wall as a place of violence and death, from the Germans "potted" as they climbed over barricades, to Nick shot and sitting immobilized against a wall, to the torero rammed against the bullring wall and pierced by the bull's horn, to the bad bullfighter symbolically castrated in front of the wall. Likewise, the images of garden and water recur meaningfully in the vignettes, and in each case the use is ironic. Water is not an element of purification and sustenance but is associated with the general terror and confusion of the Greek retreat in "Chapter II" and forms the atmospheric backdrop to the morally ambiguous executions of "Chapter V." Similarly, gardens are not centers of peaceful contemplation, nor do they connote rebirth and fertility; rather, the garden at Mons and the hospital courtyard are sites of execution, and the Greek king's garden is, for all practical purposes, a prison.

Hemingway's skill as a stylist is on concentrated display in the interchapters, where his virtuosity and innovation are put to essentially poetic use. Almost all of the vignettes can be subjected to linguistic analysis and will reveal strikingly similar results. Short declarative sentences rule the day. A word count will show a high concentration of single-syllable words, and it will also demonstrate the amazing number of repetitions that Hemingway worked into his fictions without falling into annoying mannerism. With a few purposeful exceptions, those relatively few sentences that are not grammatically simple will contain coordinated clauses rather than subordination. Sound, the purist province of the poet, is also put to use. For example, the description of Villalta's triumph in "Chapter XII" is laden with poetic sound effects. The first paragraph emphasizes Villalta's mastery and determination by using words that concentrate the *l*, *f*, *s*, and *w* sounds: "Villalta," "snarl," "bull," "firmly," "following," "feet firm," "when," "wind," "swing," and "swung." In the second paragraph *l* continues to carry this sense: "Villalta," "kill," "called," and "bull." And, as Wendolyn Tetlow has pointed out, *f* and *s* sounds "give the prose a movement like the smoothness of the bullfighter's movements": "front," "from," "folds," and "sword," "sighted," and "same" (42).[3] In each paragraph alliterated pairs emphasize Villalta's will to dominate: "feet firmly," "standing straight," and his eventual success: "sword sticking." Individual sentences embody an attention to sound equivalent to that devoted by a poet to the poetic line. The final sentence, for example, uses variations on the vowel *o* as well as the consonant *l* to emphasize the bull's defeat: "Villalta, his hand up at the crowd and the bull roaring blood, looking straight at Villalta and his legs caving."

The interchapters remain, then, a multifaced entity. They serve as a *locus classicus* for the early style, the first chance for a wider public to see the work issuing from the Hemingway expatriate atelier. They show Hemingway as a methodological groundbreaker in the field of fiction writing, as a much more experimental writer than he is often given credit for being. (While the variety of Hemingway's later fictional forms and the boundary pushing that he did as an older man have been under-recognized, this volume is his most insistently experimental in form.) As he himself indicated, the interchapters also carry the burden of delineating the larger historical context of "our time," in which the stories occur. In relationship to each other and to the various stories, they create thematic resonance and develop important continuities within the volume. Conversely, as we have just seen, they are also the most experimental aspect of the book, lending it a fragmented nature analogous to synthetic cubism. Connections and continuities exist, even though the volume looks and feels quite discontinuous.

[3] Although I have made one minor correction, I am also indebted to Tetlow for her observations about the first paragraph, and in a more general sense for the close attention she has given the poetic use of sound in this vignette (42).

6: *In Our Time* and Hemingway's Later Work

The Future of Nick Adams

WHILE *IN OUR TIME* was the public's introduction to Nick Adams, his life on the page was far from over after the publication of the volume, despite what even so perceptive a reviewer as D. H. Lawrence may have said on that subject:

> [*In Our Time*] is a short book: and it does not pretend to be about one man. But it is. It is as much as we need to know of the man's life.... And these few sketches are enough to create the man and all his history: we need no more. (93)

Hemingway still had need of Nick, and Hemingway's readership responded positively to the continuation of his chronicle. Bearing in mind that even the most directly autobiographical of Hemingway's fictions contain a great deal of pure invention and are always subject to the shaping power of the author, it is still fair to say that Nick became the most consistently autobiographical of Hemingway's protagonists, the one who was most often made to relive a fictionalized version of Hemingway's first-hand experience, the character made to feel most directly the particular pains that the author himself had felt. He remained a character to whom Hemingway even attempted to return in the 1950s, when, off and on, he worked on a Nick manuscript that was headed for novel length. "The Last Good Country" was never finished, though an edited version has been published posthumously in *The Nick Adams Stories*. But despite what this late attempt may say about the older Hemingway's desire to retain Nick as a viable character, in truth he was not a character who aged along with his creator. The published Nick Adams stories were written before Hemingway turned thirty-five, and nearly all of them depict Nick as child, adolescent, or young adult. None can be construed as taking him past early middle age.

The significance of Hemingway's inability to finish "The Last Good Country" is open to debate. On the one hand, it may reveal that he could no longer write to his own satisfaction about the youthful days of his first important character. Vivid as the adolescent world of that story may have been in his imagination (and the text does contain stretches of vintage Hemingway, despite several salient implausibilities), and compelling as the themes may have seemed to him, too much water had passed under the bridge for Hemingway to know exactly how to write this story. He could not go back. Then, too, Hemingway was working on the story during a decade when he experienced increasing trouble finishing many writing jobs on any manner of subject, so the choice of Nick as a youthful protagonist may not have been the determining obstacle that he could not surmount. Brute physiological and psychological factors eventually overmastered the skill, desire, and discipline that Hemingway did his best to summon.

Although Hemingway's final attempt to write about Nick Adams was abortive, he did remain an important character in the two volumes of short stories published subsequent to *In Our Time,* appearing several times in both *Men Without Women* (1927) and *Winner Take Nothing.*[1] To talk about the future of Nick, however, is mostly to invoke his past, for in many subsequent stories Hemingway went back in time, filling in the gaps, narrating events that occurred prior to "Big Two-Hearted River." Three of these stories go far toward explaining Nick's frame of mind in that work, for they deal explicitly with Nick's wounding in the war, his hospitalization, his slow recovery, and, most important, the mental instability from which he suffered while still in wartime Italy. "In Another Country" seems to elaborate the aftermath of the wounding Nick receives in "Chapter VI." It depicts the ruined lives of wounded soldiers in a hospital, in

---

[1] The inexact word *several* must be used because both volumes contain stories narrated by an anonymous first-person narrator who may with good reason be construed as Nick Adams but cannot incontrovertibly be proven to be Nick.

hospital, in particular the physical therapy of the American narrator and an Italian major.[2] It is clear that the physical therapy is useless and that some sort of spiritual therapy would be more valuable for the psychically battered men. "Now I Lay Me" depicts Nick and an Italian soldier lying awake at night near the front, unable to sleep. Nick dreads sleeping because he fears that his soul will leave his body. "A Way You'll Never Be" has Nick returning to the Italian front to do some public relations work and morale boosting among the Italian soldiers; but this proves to be a ridiculous assignment, for he has received a serious head wound and can scarcely control himself. Indeed, his day-to-day focus is not on fulfilling his military duties but on maintaining his tenuous grip on his sanity. These three war stories were composed after the publication of *In Our Time,* and they are among Hemingway's best work. They are of interest for their high degree of autobiographical resonance, as well as for the light they shed on *A Farewell to Arms* and on each other. Most to the point here, however, is their resonance with *In Our Time.* We should recall the moment in "The Battler" when Ad reports to Bugs of young Nick that "He says he's never been crazy." Bugs replies dryly that "He's got a lot coming to him" (57). Thus, what is alluded to in "Big Two-Hearted River," the submerged part of the iceberg, is fleshed out in these subsequently published stories. It is clear that Nick has come in for his full share of beatings courtesy of the war. Bugs's words about losing one's mind have been fulfilled.

Other subsequent stories deal with Nick's youth. "Ten Indians" anticipates the more serious sense of loss that the older Nick feels in "The End of Something." In it the still boyish Nick is heartbroken over a betrayal by Prudie, a Native American whom he apparently considered his exclusive girlfriend but whom Nick's father has seen

---

[2] I say "*seems to* elaborate" because there is no absolute proof that the nameless narrator of this fine story is Nick, and there is some inconclusive evidence that might be offered to show that he is not Nick. There are, however, so many important similarities between the narrator and Nick Adams that at the very least it is safe to grant "In Another Country" the status of being what Joseph DeFalco has termed a "generic Nick Adams" story.

"threshing around" amorously in the woods with another boy. "The Killers" is a frightening story that, while not as rich, can be considered a companion piece to "The Battler." In each story Nick seems to be in his mid or late teens, in each he is given a sudden and unprovoked experience of violence, and in each a retired prizefighter figures as a beleaguered character. In "The Killers" Nick again has violence done to him, again he is threatened with still worse violence than he actually receives, and again he sees how utterly and quickly the world can take a man down. In "Fathers and Sons" Nick, grown up with a son of his own, reminisces about his father, remembering him fondly for his keen eyesight and skill as a hunter and more ruefully for his inadequate and moralistic "explanations" of sex. He remembers his own initial sexual relationship with Trudy, an Indian girl from northern Michigan (Prudie seems to have been transformed into Trudy with the passage of a few years), and he remembers also his minor disgusts and his adolescent fury with his father. The story ends with Nick's son asking to be taken to visit Dr. Adams's grave, a trip Nick avoids firmly committing himself to making.

Finally, a number of post-*In Our Time* stories that are narrated by anonymous first persons could more or less plausibly be considered Nick Adams stories. I have already mentioned "In Another Country" in this light, and the evidence is also compelling that Nick narrates "The Light of the World" (one of Hemingway's self-declared favorites among his works) and "An Alpine Idyll." Less likely is the slighter "A Day's Wait," another father-son story. Even less likely, though still plausible, is "Wine of Wyoming," a story Hemingway seems to have conceived with large ambition but that falls comparatively flat. Comic and snide and full of literary allusions, "The Light of the World" contributes to the picture of Nick's adolescent years. With its open description of a conversation among prostitutes (the word *whores* is used in the story) and its references to homosexuality, it must have shocked Hemingway's parents and other staid Oak Parkers. If "The Battler" and "The Killers" serve as Nick's introduction to violence, his experiences in "The Light of the World" make clear many things that Dr. Adams had not wanted to teach him about sex. "An Alpine Idyll" is one of Hemingway's ventures into absurdist writing and black humor, written long before those terms had literary currency. It is the story of a half-witted man who murders his wife, stores her body in the barn all winter, and hangs a lantern from her frozen-stiff mouth. The narrator is an American on a European skiing trip, and the story can be read as a complementary piece to "Cross-Country Snow."

The Future of a Form: *In Our Time* and the Later Works

While Nick Adams had a noteworthy life after *In Our Time,* the more extreme aspects of the book's experimental vein did not. Hemingway's next book was *The Torrents of Spring* (1926), an extended exercise in parody that was written largely as a contract breaker.[3] Then came the two fame-making novels, *The Sun Also Rises* and *A Farewell to Arms,* both of which break new fictional ground and are bold works in their own way, but neither of which embodies the more aggressive experiments in form found in *In Our Time.* Each novel advanced Hemingway's reputation as a trademark stylist, with the former hewing more closely to the hallmarks we have already discussed in relation to *In Our Time.* In particular, Hemingway's skill at creating terse but heavily suggestive conversation was developed to its fullest potential in *The Sun Also Rises,* as was his Cézanne-like method of blocking out the countryside in descriptive passages of sheer virtuosity. But neither of these novels — and, indeed, nothing that came after *In Our Time* — would have the fractured, cubist quality of that book.

A devoted experimenter with narrative forms himself, William Faulkner once said that of his great contemporaries Hemingway had dared the least — a statement that would seem to overlook the experiments in genre represented by *Death in the Afternoon* and *Green Hills of Africa;* the accomplished stream-of-consciousness narration to be found in "The Snows of Kilimanjaro," among other fictions; and the thematic and formal boundary-pushing to be found in the posthumous works. (About the last, of course, Faulkner had no way of knowing. *A Moveable Feast,* to take just one example, can be said to anticipate by some forty years the recent spate of literarily in-

---

[3] The details of this stratagem can be found in any of the recent full-length biographies.

tended, highly fictionalized memoirs, a form under much discussion in the last few years for its supposed novelty.) Nevertheless, in regard to the complexity of formal structuring, Faulkner's statement has merit. Perhaps Faulkner — who was, after all, the most aggressively avant-garde American formalist writing in an avant-garde era — had in mind the relative traditionalism in terms of internal construction that Hemingway displayed subsequent to *In Our Time*.

Although he had been working hard for what must have seemed to him a long time, Hemingway's career was, of course, just beginning in 1925. It is easy to lose sight of that fact when reading this impressive volume. If it seems remarkable how quickly Hemingway rose to this stage in his career, the next five years would prove truly phenomenal. In the following year *The Sun Also Rises* gave Hemingway a commercial success, a greater notoriety both within and without the Paris writers' scene, and increasing attention from influential critics. It also cemented his long-term relationship with editor Maxwell Perkins and his lifetime partnership with the Scribner's publishing house. *A Farewell to Arms* came out in 1929, making Hemingway a wealthy man and a world-famous figure. Hemingway as artist had proved himself. Hemingway as celebrity was launched.[4]

Much of what makes these subsequent books successful can be found in *In Our Time*. While it does not exhibit the experimental spirit displayed in that book's form, Hemingway's immediately subsequent work does embody the core values that are at the heart of his so-called Code. These core values are already largely present in the early volume, sometimes incipiently. Subsequent books would flesh out these values, show the Code in action. The oeuvre's continuity, then, is to be found in Hemingway's themes and not in the experimental form of *In Our Time*.

---

[4] John Raeburn and Scott Donaldson ("Hemingway and Fame") provide insightful treatments of the interplay between Hemingway's career as a writer and his ever-growing celebrity. Leonard J. Leff approaches the topic with an emphasis on Hemingway's relationship to Hollywood and the media culture of the 1930s.

Hemingway as Traditionalist

In fact, Hemingway's core values show a strong strain of traditionalism. Gertrude Stein sensed this fact early, turning Hemingway's traditionalism against him in an insult that imputed a falseness at the heart of her one-time tyro: "He looks like a modern and he smells of the museums," she said in her *Autobiography of Alice B. Toklas* (1933), a book that aims several sharp elbows at Hemingway (266). But there was nothing false either in Hemingway's modernist tendencies or in his traditionalism. The one did not set out to disguise the other or merely to paint it over with a thin coat. Seventy-five years later, no knowledgeable reader would argue that Hemingway did not revolutionize the language of fiction; nor can anyone reading *In Our Time* conclude that Hemingway, especially as a young man, was not fully engaged in his times. Often he did not like what he saw, but disapproval is quite a different matter from mere disengagement. "He had seen the world change," the semi-autobiographical and self-castigating protagonist, Harry, thinks of himself in "The Snows of Kilimanjaro"; "not just the events; although he had seen many of them and had watched the people, but he had seen the subtler change and he could remember how the people were at different times. He had been in it and he had watched it and it was his duty to write of it" (*The Short Stories* 66). *In Our Time* marks the beginning of Hemingway's register of both the gross and, especially, the "subtler" aspects of modern life. At the same time, buried in that register, or perhaps undergirding its foundations, is a set of core values that can fairly be called "traditional."

Not all of these traditional values are fully developed in *In Our Time;* some are barely introduced, to be worked out more fully in subsequent fictions. For one thing, none of the important characters in the stories proper of *In Our Time* is very old. Those who are over twenty-five — Dr. Adams, Ad Francis, Joe Butler's father — share the stage with Nick or some other character of at least equal importance to themselves. The significant adult characters here are weak and wounded, much closer to defeat than to victory. Some have learned how to cope, some how to survive, some how to barely hang on, but none has come near to achieving the sort of actualization of a positive, self-directed set of principles that would signify the later characters that Hemingway intended as admirable figures.

But we do see these principles in embryonic form. In "Big Two-Hearted River," when Nick wets his hands before unhooking the fish he intends to throw back, we see what Hemingway's later texts will reaffirm: that one must discover on one's own what is worth caring about and working to preserve and then be loyal to that venture. We see the positive principles in Nick's declaration of a "separate peace" in "Chapter VI," a creative seed that would flower into *A Farewell to Arms.* One need not depend on grand causes or great institutions; in fact, one had better not invest much of oneself in them. Armies, churches, governments, families — all are more apt to mislead, to constrain, or to serve themselves than to serve the individual or give meaning to his life. We see what some foundational critics would later call the Hemingway Code sketched in miniature in "Chapter XII" in Villalta's moment of triumph, a confrontation of his own choosing, managed on terms he understands and to which he consents, set in a meaningful — indeed, ritualized — context, and executed with bravery and élan. Although the protagonists in Hemingway's two best novels — Jake Barnes in *The Sun Also Rises* and Frederic Henry in *A Farewell to Arms* — are older and more mature than Nick in *In Our Time,* they suffer equally, and both are looking for their own way to make their separate peace. They have an advantage over Nick insofar as they have the opportunity to become acquainted with men who embody a more fully developed moral sense than anyone in *In Our Time.* Count Mippipopolous, Pedro Romero, Count Greffi, the young priest in *A Farewell to Arms:* each is incomplete, each has imperfections, but each is a model for men who are trying to "learn how to live in it," as Jake declares he is trying to do.

Beneath the sensational surface of Hemingway's fiction, existing alongside his unflinching observations of the seamy, the distasteful, and the truly immoral, resides a core of values that would not have displeased his scandalized parents had they been able to understand their son's work better. It will be remembered that Hemingway's father had returned many of the copies of Ernest's early work that he had ordered. Likewise, after *The Sun Also Rises* had been discussed in her Oak Park book-study class, Grace wrote to Ernest that "every page [of it] fills me with a sick loathing" (JFK collection). She claimed to be repeating the consensus of readers in her class, and she undoubtedly *was* expressing (in the most ill-chosen words imaginable) the reaction of many offended readers. But what such readers could not see then seems clear now. Hemingway's frequent forthrightness and occasional iconoclasm were shocking, of course, and the shock effect was important in its own right, but he never intended to shock purely for the effect of shocking.

Hemingway was intent on depicting a world that was adrift precisely because so many of the old values had been forgotten or rendered untenable in the modern, postwar period.[5] But many of the old values survive in his stories, even if they are sometimes reworked to concur with the new times. It is not difficult to construct a partial list: work gives meaning to life and is one of the few things that can be counted on; a person is happiest when work and pleasure are wed; love is valuable despite the fact that it is contingent and impermanent; life confronts each man and woman with unforeseen, unasked-for tests, and the measure of the person is in how he or she handles these tests; ease and luxury must be earned and constantly balanced with accomplishment if they are to be enjoyed. The Hemingway of *In Our Time* had every desire to make it new, and he had every desire to show the world as he saw it rather than to whitewash it with deceitful wholesomeness; but he could not have embraced any nihilistic or value-free view of the world.

Hemingway at His Best

Compelling companion that Hemingway often was, even his most loyal friends report a bluster factor that surfaced with greater frequency and intensity as he grew older; and, sadly, Hemingway sometimes gave it play not only in his life but also in his work. As an older man Hemingway too frequently succumbed to the temptation to project himself into his texts; in one way or another he insisted

---

[5] Michael Reynolds has written about the hold that Hemingway's Oak Park upbringing maintained on him. See especially *The Young Hemingway*, chapters 2 ("Home as Found") and 9 ("City Lights").

too much on his expertise. Indeed, he *was* a man of remarkable experience and imposing accomplishment apart from his writing. The fierce competitive streak, which irritated some friends and also some critics, was essential to his creative makeup. But when expertise becomes imbued with condescension and complacence, when knowledge turns into knowingness, his work suffers. As early as 1941 Edmund Wilson remarked that Hemingway was "the worst invented character to be found in the author's work" (226). What would Jake Barnes have had to say about Colonel Cantwell, the windy protagonist of *Across the River and Into the Trees* (1950), had he been able to meet the latter? What would the young Hemingway who created Nick Adams have said about the older Hemingway as he shows himself in that novel? Hemingway as his own hero could be a boor in life and a bore on the page.[6]

Hemingway was at his best creating those who are needy, insufficient, caught in circumstances over which they have little control. His most compelling characters are searching for answers, not supplying them to others, let alone pontificating. In *The Sun Also Rises* Jake Barnes decides that he must forego the development of a grand philosophy and confine his hopes simply to "learning how to live in it," a phrase that could be used by Nick, or Harold Krebs, or the Revolutionist, or Joe, or the British officer, or the former king of Greece. Hemingway's finest works portray people who have been broken or who are in the process of staving off imminent collapse. That they will later become stronger at the broken part, as Frederic Henry declares in *A Farewell to Arms,* is an ennobling conception; but the fiction remains essentially tragic, depicting their defeats, not the hoped-for victories that may eventually come. The exemplary

---

[6] While it is outside the scope of this study to consider at length the impact of the posthumously published works on Hemingway's reputation, I wish to acknowledge here that they go far toward dispelling any version of Hemingway's later work as relentlessly egotistical. The self-pleased author is present in them, and occasionally even the pontifical one, but so too is the humorous, the self-deprecating, and the sly Hemingway. Though not always self-aware, he was much more so at all stages of his career than his more astringent critics would allow.

characters in the best fictions, those who have come out on the other side, show their expertise or their joi de vivre in what they do and in how they do it, not in what they say. They often teach by example; and when they do teach with words, the words are gently or playfully instructional, not insistent or self-important.

One essential difference between the adolescent Nick whom Hemingway was creating in the unfinished "Last Good Country," on the one hand, and the Nick of *In Our Time* and the subsequent stories from the 1930s, on the other hand, is that Nick is a victim in the early stories. In "The Last Good Country," though Hemingway undoubtedly planned on writing the story of a lost Eden, a sort of anti-idyll wherein Nick eventually does get caught, there seems to be nothing that Nick does not know or cannot take care of and no one whom he cannot outsmart. Only time and space will eventually defeat him. He knows full well how to outmaneuver everyone and run away. The problem will not be with Nick's limitations; rather, he will lose in the end only because there will not be enough land to which he can escape. Also, at the risk of sounding moralistic, I would assert that in "The Last Good Country" Nick has done wrong of his own volition for essentially petty and selfish — if not downright delinquent — reasons, and this fact lessens the reader's sympathy for him. Here again, the less attractive side of Hemingway comes into view. As an older man, Hemingway was known to invent tales about his youth that made it seem much wilder and outside-the-law than it actually had been. Undoubtedly these stories fed into the tough-guy image that appeared important to one side of Hemingway; but when this impulse was transferred to his fiction without the necessary awareness of its aura of wish fulfillment, the fiction suffered, just as it did when the "expert" Hemingway showed up or showed off too directly. Nick remains a much more compelling character when he is knocked about by circumstances, as he is in the fictions of *In Our Time*.

Readers of this early volume today must feel, besides their present pleasures and puzzlements, a retrospective excitement. History has made it clear that we are reading the already rich and accomplished stories of a determined, strong-willed, and exuberant young master who was on the cusp of literary stardom. I expect that this book will continue to stand up as well as any of Hemingway's best volumes — as well, even, as his most frequently read novels — so that on the bicentennial of its author's birth it will remain the rich source of puzzlement and awakening, of aggravation and satisfaction, that it was in the year of the first centenary, just concluded.

Works Cited

Baker, Carlos. *Ernest Hemingway: A Life Story.* New York: Scribner's, 1969.

———. *Hemingway: The Writer as Artist,* fourth edition. Princeton, NJ: Princeton UP, 1972.

Beegel, Susan F. *Hemingway's Craft of Omission: Four Manuscript Examples.* Ann Arbor, MI: UMI Research Press, 1988.

Benson, Jackson J. "Patterns of Connection and Their Development in Hemingway's *In Our Time*" (1970). Reprinted in *Critical Essays on Ernest Hemingway's* In Our Time, edited by Michael Reynolds. Boston: G. K. Hall, 1983, 103–119.

Bloom, Harold, ed. *Ernest Hemingway.* Modern Critical Views series. New York: Chelsea House, 1985.

Brasch, James, and Joseph Sigmund. *Hemingway's Library.* Boston: Hall, 1981.

Brogan, Jacqueline Vaught. "Hemingway's *In Our Time:* A Cubist Anatomy," *Hemingway Review* 17.2 (Spring 1998): 31–46.

Bruccoli, Matthew J., ed. *The Only Thing That Counts: The Ernest Hemingway/Maxwell Perkins Correspondence, 1925–1947.* New York: Scribner's, 1996.

Carpenter, Humphrey. *Geniuses Together: American Writers in Paris in the 1920s.* Boston: Houghton Mifflin, 1988.

Cohen, Milton. "Attacking the Home Front: World War I and Rebelliousness in Hemingway, Dos Passos, and Cummings." Paper delivered at the Ernest Hemingway Centennial Literary Conference, Oak Park, IL, July 1999.

Comley, Nancy R., and Robert Scholes. *Hemingway's Genders: Rereading the Hemingway Text.* New Haven, CT: Yale UP, 1994.

DeFalco, Joseph. *The Hero in Hemingway's Short Stories.* Pittsburgh: U of Pittsburgh P, 1963.

Donaldson, Scott, ed. *The Cambridge Companion to Hemingway*. New York: Cambridge UP, 1996.

——. "Introduction: Hemingway and Fame," *in The Cambridge Companion to Hemingway*. New York: Cambridge UP, 1996.

Fenton, Charles A. *The Apprenticeship of Ernest Hemingway*. New York: Farrar, Straus & Young, 1954.

Flora, Joseph M. *Ernest Hemingway: A Study of the Short Fiction*. Boston: Twayne, 1989.

Groseclose, Barbara. "Hemingway's 'The Revolutionist': An Aid to Interpretation," *Modern Fiction Studies* 17 (1971–1972): 565–570.

Hagemann, E. R. "'Only Let the Story End as Soon as Possible': Time-and-History in Ernest Hemingway's *In Our Time*." 1980. Reprinted in *Critical Essays on Ernest Hemingway's* In Our Time, edited by Michael Reynolds. Boston: Hall, 1983, 52–60.

Hemingway, Ernest. *Across the River and Into the Trees*. New York: Scribner's, 1950.

——. "The Art of the Short Story," *Paris Review* 23 (Spring 1981): 85–102.

——. *Death in the Afternoon*. New York: Scribner's, 1932.

——. *A Farewell to Arms*. New York: Scribner's, 1929.

——. *For Whom the Bell Tolls*. New York: Scribner's, 1940.

——. *The Garden of Eden*. New York: Scribner's, 1986.

——. *Green Hills of Africa*. New York: Scribner's, 1935.

——. *in our time*. Paris: Three Mountains Press, 1924; reprinted Columbia, S.C.: Bruccoli Clark, 1977.

——. *In Our Time*. New York: Boni & Liveright, 1925; revised edition, New York: Scribner's, 1930; republished, New York: Scribner's, 1970. The 1970 edition is the standard paperback edition; as a convenience to the reader, it is cited in the present study. At the time of publication of this study, the current paperback printing retains the pagination of this edition.

——. *Men Without Women*. New York: Scribner's, 1927.

——. *A Moveable Feast*. New York: Scribner's, 1964.

——. *The Nick Adams Stories,* edited by Philip Young. New York: Scribner's, 1972.

——. *Selected Letters, 1917–1961,* edited by Carlos Baker. New York: Scribner's, 1981.

——. *The Sun Also Rises.* New York: Scribner's, 1926.

——. *The Short Stories of Ernest Hemingway: The First Forty-Nine Stories.* 1938. New York: MacMillan in the Scribner Classics/Collier Edition Series, 1986.

——. *The Torrents of Spring.* New York: Scribner's, 1926.

——. *Winner Take Nothing.* New York: Scribner's, 1933.

Hermann, Thomas. "Formal Analogies in the Texts and Paintings of Ernest Hemingway and Paul Cézanne," in *Hemingway Repossessed,* edited by Kenneth Rosen. Westport, CT: Praeger, 1994, 29–33.

Hunt, Anthony. "Another Turn for Hemingway's 'The Revolutionist': Sources and Meanings," in *Critical Essays on Ernest Hemingway's In Our Time,* edited by Michael Reynolds. Boston: Hall, 1983, 203–217.

Imamura, Tateo. "'Soldier's Home': Another Story of a Broken Heart," *The Hemingway Review* 16.1 (Fall 1996): 102–107.

Johnston, Kenneth G. *The Tip of the Iceberg: Hemingway and the Short Story.* Greenwood, FL: Penkevill, 1987.

Kazin, Alfred. "Hemingway the Painter," in his *An American Procession: The Major American Writers from 1830–1930 — The Crucial Century.* 1984. Republished, New York: Vintage Books, 1985, 357–373.

Kenner, Hugh. *A Homemade World: The American Modernist Writers.* New York: Knopf, 1975, especially 119–157.

Lawrence, D. H. "*In Our Time*: A Review." 1925. Reprinted in *Hemingway: A Collection of Critical Essays,* edited by Robert P. Weeks. Twentieth Century Views series. Englewood Cliffs, NJ: Prentice-Hall, 1962, 93-94.

Leff, Leonard J. *Hemingway and His Conspirators: Hollywood, Scribner's and the Making of American Celebrity Culture.* Lanham, MD: Rowman & Littlefield, 1997.

Levin, Harry. "Observations on the Style of Ernest Hemingway." 1957. Reprinted in *Ernest Hemingway,* edited by Harold Bloom. Modern Critical Views series. New York: Chelsea House, 1985, 54–66.

Lewis, Robert W., Jr. "Hemingway's Concept of Sport and 'Soldier's Home.'" *Rendezvous* 5 (Winter 1970): 19–27.

Lynn, Kenneth S. *Hemingway.* New York: Simon & Schuster, 1987.

MacLeish, Archibald. "Years of the Dog," in his *Actfive and Other Poems.* 1948. Republished in his *Collected Poems, 1917–1982.* Boston: Houghton Mifflin, 1985.

Mann, Susan Garland. "Ernest Hemingway's *In Our Time,*" in her *The Short Story Cycle: A Genre Companion and Reference Guide.* New York: Greenwood Press, 1989, 71–91.

Mellow, James R. *Hemingway: A Life without Consequences.* Boston: Houghton Mifflin, 1992.

Meyers, Jeffrey. *Hemingway: A Biography.* New York: Harper and Row, 1985.

Moddlemog, Debra. "The Unifying Consciousness of a Divided Conscience: Nick Adams as Author of *In Our Time,*" *American Literature* 60 (December 1988): 591–610.

Raeburn, John. *Fame Became of Him: Hemingway as Public Writer.* Bloomington: Indiana UP, 1984.

Reynolds, Michael. *Hemingway's First War: The Making of* A Farewell to Arms. Princeton, NJ: Princeton UP, 1976.

——. "Hemingway's *In Our Time:* The Biography of a Book," in *Modern American Short Story Sequences,* edited by J. Gerald Kennedy. New York: Cambridge UP, 1995, 35–51.

——. *Hemingway's Reading, 1910–1940.* Princeton, NJ: Princeton UP, 1981.

——. *Hemingway: The American Homecoming.* Cambridge, MA: Blackwell, 1992.

——. *Hemingway: The Final Years.* New York: Norton, 1999.

——. *Hemingway: The Paris Years.* Cambridge, MA: Blackwell, 1989.

——. *Hemingway: The 1930s.* New York: Norton, 1997.

——. *The Young Hemingway.* New York: Blackwell, 1986.

——. ed. *Critical Essays on Ernest Hemingway's* In Our Time. Boston: Hall, 1983.

Rosen, Kenneth, ed. *Hemingway Repossessed*. Westport, CT: Praeger, 1994.

Rovit, Earl, and Gerry Brenner. *Ernest Hemingway*, revised edition. Boston: Twayne, 1986.

Smith, Paul. *A Reader's Guide to the Short Stories of Ernest Hemingway*. Boston: Hall, 1989.

Stein, Gertrude. *The Autobiography of Alice B. Toklas*. 1933. Republished, New York: Vintage Books, 1961.

Stevens, Wallace. *Letters of Wallace Stevens*, edited by Holly Stevens. New York: Knopf, 1981.

Strychacz, Thomas. "*In Our Time*, Out of Season," in *The Cambridge Companion to Hemingway*, edited by Scott Donaldson. New York: Cambridge UP, 1996, 87–108.

Tetlow, Wendolyn. *Hemingway's* In Our Time: *Lyrical Dimensions*. Lewisburg, PA: Bucknell UP, 1992.

Vaughn, Elizabeth Dewberry. "*In Our Time* and Picasso," in *Hemingway Repossessed*, edited by Kenneth Rosen. Westport, CT: Praeger, 1994, 3–8.

Villard, Henry S., and James Nagel, eds. *Hemingway in Love and War: The Lost Diary of Agnes von Kurowsky, Her Letters, and Correspondence of Ernest Hemingway*. Boston: Northeastern UP, 1989.

Wilson, Edmund. "Hemingway: Gauge of Morale," in his *The Wound and the Bow*. Boston: Houghton Mifflin, 1941, 214–242.

Index

In Our Time was Ernest Hemingway's first commercial publication. Its appearance in 1925 launched the full-fledged literary career of this century's most famous American fiction writer. *Modernism and Tradition in Ernest Hemingway's "In Our Time": A Guide for Students and Readers* is a well-paced, lucidly written handbook intended to help the inquisitive reader gain a better understanding of Hemingway's complex, still-puzzling first volume. It provides a useful road map to Hemingway's complex modernist master-piece and is aimed at the reader who is not already a specialist in the field of Hemingway studies. University students will find the book especially useful, as will faculty who are teaching the work.

All fifteen stories and sixteen vignettes found in *In Our Time* receive a critical reading without sacrificing a sense of the book as a whole. Indeed, this study stresses the status of *In Our Time* as a discrete volume, a master-work in its own right, worthy of a place alongside *The Sun Also Rises* and *A Farewell to Arms*. Stewart considers the book as a distinctly modern literary form, finding that none of Hemingway's subsequent works would again carry the degree of modernist experimentation found here.

Thus Stewart examines at length *In Our Time's* status as a modernist achievement, and the book includes considerations of Hemingway's prose styles, his theories of writing, his formal intentions for the volume, his lite-rary mentors and influences. Stewart examines the tension between Hem-ingway's modernist, experimental impulses and the traditionalist core that remains even in this, his most radical work. Stewart also focuses attention on the much-debated formal status of this collection of fictions, and considers biographical and historical events that had a direct bearing on the fiction. Finally *In Our Time* is placed in relation to later works by Hemingway, both those that grow out of it, and those that do not.

Matthew C. Stewart is Associate Professor of Humanities and Rhetoric at Boston University.

Lightning Source UK Ltd.
Milton Keynes UK
UKHW011835090821
388576UK00001B/45